Collins

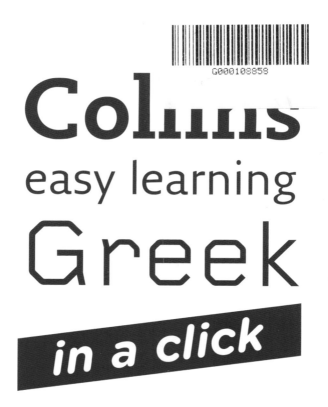

easy learning Greek

in a click

Emmanuela Pantelireis

HarperCollins Publishers
77-85 Fulham Palace Road
London W6 8JB
Great Britain

www.collinslanguage.com

First edition 2010

Reprint 10 9 8 7 6 5 4 3 2 1

ISBN 978-0-00-733714-9

A catalogue record for this book is available from the British Library

Typeset by Q2AMedia

Cover image courtesy of Corbis

Audio material recorded and produced by Networks SRL, Milan

Printed and Bound in China by Leo Paper Products Ltd.

Editorial Director: Eva Martinez

Series Editor: Rob Scriven

Contents

Introduction

Welcome to *Collins Easy Learning Greek in a Click*. This is a new course which aims to give you all the skills you'll need to start understanding and using Greek quickly, easily and effectively in real situations.

This course is aimed at adult learners with no previous experience of Greek. We've thought about which situations would be most useful to you during a visit to Greece, and have created a course that embraces all the main scenarios a traveller would be likely to encounter, such as public transport, checking into a hotel, shopping, eating out and visiting a museum. There's a section on keeping in touch using your computer or phone, and also a unit devoted to finding your way around and asking for help if anything goes wrong.

Our approach is not to bombard you with too much grammar, but rather to let you listen to authentic dialogues set in useful situations, giving you the nuts and bolts of what's being said, then guiding you through carefully gauged practice exercises to increase your confidence.

The tools you need to succeed

The course has been designed to provide you with three essential tools in order to make your language learning experience a success. In your pack you'll find an activation code for the **online course**, this handy **book**, and an **audio CD**. You can use a combination of these whenever and wherever you are, making the course work for you.

The online course

www.collinslanguage.com/click provides you with a 12-unit online interactive language experience. Listen to a dialogue (and follow the words on-screen if you like) then study the new words and phrases before tackling some fun interactive games and exercises. You'll then also have the chance to perfect your pronunciation by recording your own voice (microphone not provided).

Your progress will be saved automatically as you advance through the course in order that every time you log in you can see how well you've done in each of the exercises and how much of the course you've completed so far. If at any point you want to improve on your original scores, you can always go back and have another go.

To access the online course simply go to www.collinslanguage.com/click and enter your personal activation code which you will find inside the front cover of this book.

The book

There will be times when it's not practical for you to be at a computer. There will also be times when you simply don't want to stare at the screen. For these times, this pocket-sized book contains the whole course for you in a handy portable format, so you can continue learning without the need for a computer. All of the content you need to learn Greek is right here in this book. Study the language and complete the exercises just as you would online.

When you want to check your answers, go to **www.collinslanguage.com/click** to download the answer key.

The audio CD

Use the audio CD to hear native Greek speakers engaging in dialogues set in real life situations and use it alongside the book in order to improve your listening comprehension skills. The audio CD can be downloaded to your mp3 player so that you can keep on learning even when you're on the move.

See the website at **www.collinslanguage.com/click** for the written transcript of all the spoken dialogues.

How it works

Greek in a Click is divided into 12 units. Each unit begins with a **Traveller's tip**, a short passage highlighting an area of Greek life and culture. This mini-section sets the scene for the rest of the unit.

Following a brief summary of the language structures you're about to study, we move straight on to the first dialogue, headed **Listen up**. Any tricky or useful vocabulary is explained in the accompanying **Words and phrases** box (with accompanying audio online), then we go into a little more detail in **Unlocking the language**. Then it's over to you. **Your Turn** offers further practice of each structure and area of vocabulary encountered.

Halfway through each unit, you'll see that the cycle begins again with a fresh **Listen up**. This adds a different dimension to the material and scenario you've already looked at, and provides you with a new challenge in a slightly different situation. The range of exercises and practical tips continues throughout.

Each unit ends with **Let's Recap**, in which you can check over the language you've used in the unit and make sure you can reproduce certain key words and expressions from memory. The online version then gives you the chance to record yourself saying some of the most important vocabulary from the unit, to compare your pronunciation with that of a native speaker.

***Collins Easy Learning Greek in a Click* aims to be fun, but at the same time to equip you with genuinely useful linguistic and cultural tools to make the most of your time in Greece. We hope you enjoy it!**

Pronunciation Guide

To make it as clear as possible how to pronounce the Greek in this book, we've supplied a phonetic transliteration below of some example words. We use bold letters for Greek words and then italic for the transliterations, with underlining to show either how each letter is pronounced or where each word should be stressed.

Greek pronunciation is not difficult and unlike English has the advantage of being predictable and logical. Once you have learnt the alphabet and a few basic rules, it shouldn't be too long before you can read straight from the Greek without bothering with the transliteration.

The vowels are very straightforward. There are seven simple and five two-letter vowels and each one has just one sound, unlike in English.

Simple and two-letter vowels

Greek	sounds like	example	transliteration
α	**a**pple	**άλογο**	*alogho*
ε, αι	p**e**n	**Ελλάδα**	*Elladha*
		αίμα	*ema*
η, ι, υ, ει, οι	**i**nk	**ήλιος**	*eeleeos*
		Ιταλία	*Eetaleea*
		υπόγειο	*eepogheeo*
		είκοσι	*eekosee*
		μεγάλοι	*meghalee*
ο, ω	p**o**t	**όμιλος**	*omeelos*
		εγώ	*egho*
ου	l**oo**k	**ουρανός**	*ooranos*

As you may have noticed, there are five different vowels – **η, ι, υ, ει, οι** – with the same 'ee' sound. It is not always possible to know which 'ee' letter should be in the beginning or in the middle of a word. On the other hand, there are some simple rules to follow which will help you write the correct 'ee' at the end:

η This is the feminine definite article in the nominative singular. Example: **η πόρτα**/*ee porta*/the door
All feminine words that end in 'ee', end in **–η** (*eeta*). Example: **η αδελφή**/*ee adhelfee*/the sister

ι Neuter words ending in 'ee', end in **–ι** (*gheeota*). Example: **το παιδί**/*to pedhee*/the child

υ υ (eepseelon) can be the ending of some masculine and neuter adjectives, such as μακρύς/*makrees*/μακρύ/*makree*/long or πολύς/*polees*/πολύ/*polee*/ many

ει When conjugating a verb -εις and -ει will be the endings for the second and third persons singular. Example: γράφεις/*ghrafees*/you write, and γράφει/ *ghrafee*/he or she writes

οι This is the definite article in the nominative plural for both masculine and feminine words.
Example: οι άντρες/*ee andres*/the men, οι μητέρες/*ee meeteres*/the mothers. It is also the plural ending for both masculine and feminine words ending in -ος. Example: ο φίλος/οι φίλοι/*ee feelee*, η έξοδος/οι έξοδοι/*ee eksodhee*.

We also have two different letters: ο (*ommeekron*) and ω (*omegha*) for the 'o' sound. You normally use -ο as a neuter ending. Example: αυγό/*avgho*/egg and -ω as a verb ending or an adverb ending. Example: παίζω/*pezo*/play, εδώ/*edho*/here

There are also two different letters – ε, αι – for the 'e' sound. You use -αι as a reflexive verb ending. Example: Κοιμάμαι/*keemame*/I sleep, Κοιμάσαι/*keemase*/you sleep, etc.

Consonants

Greek	**sounds like**	**example**	**transliteration**
β	**v**ery	βάρκα	*varka*
γ	**y**es	γιατρός	*gheeatros*
δ	**th**is	δέντρο	*dhendro*
ζ	**z**oo	ζώνη	*zonee*
θ	**th**in	θάρρος	*tharos*
κ	**k**ey	κεντρί	*kendree*
λ	**l**emon	λεμόνι	*lemonee*
μ	**m**ask	μάσκα	*maska*
ν	**n**ame	νερό	*nero*
ξ	ne**x**t	ξύδι	*kseedhee*
π	**p**aper	πόλη	*polee*
ρ	**r**ing	ρόδα	*rodha*
σ, ς	**s**ong	σήμα	*seema*
τ	**t**ea	τέλος	*telos*
φ	**f**ox	φίδι	*feedhee*
χ	lo**ch**	χέρι	*kheree*
ψ	la**ps**	ψάρι	*psaree*

In Greek we don't have a single letter for the sounds 'b' and 'd'. We need to combine two letters: μπ = 'b' and ντ = 'd'.

Equally, we don't have sounds such as 'sh' or 'ch'. That's why Greek people find it hard to pronounce words such as 'shop' or 'church'. They will say '*sop*' and '*tserts*'.

For the letter 'j' we have τζ. Example: τζάκι/*tzakee*/fireplace. And for 'g' we have γκ and γγ. Example: γκαράζ/*garaz*/garage, Αγγλία/*Angleea*/England.

Note: We never start a word with γγ.

Sometimes certain letter sounds such as 'σ', 'ν' and 'γ' change depending on the letters following them. The letter sound 'σ' changes to 'z' when followed directly by β, γ, δ, λ, μ, ν, ρ, μπ and ντ or by a word starting with one of the above letters. Example: Σμύρνη/*zmeernee*/Smyrna, σγουρά/*zghoora*/curly, σβήνω/*zveeno*/to switch off, Στις δέκα/*Steez dheka*/at ten.

When the letter 'γ' is followed by 'χ' then its sound changes to 'ν'. Example: συγχρόνως/*seenkhronos*/simultaneously

If a word starting with κ, π or τ is preceded by a word ending in 'ν', then the letters κ, π and τ sound '*ng*', '*nb*', '*nd*'.
Example: δεν κοιμάμαι/*dhen Geemame*/I am not sleeping, στην Πάτρα/*steen Batra*/ in Patras, στην ταβέρνα/*steen daverna*/at the taverna.

Combinations

αυ, ευ are pronounced *af* and *ef* if they are followed by γκ, κ, ξ, π, σ, τ, φ, χ.
Example: αυτοκίνητο/*aftokeeneeto*/car, αύξηση/*afkseesee*/increase

αυ, ευ are pronounced *av* and *ev* if they are followed by β, γ, δ, λ, μ, ν, ρ. Example: αυγό/*avgho*/egg, αυλή/*avlee*/courtyard

αί and αι are 'e' sounds and οί and οι are 'ee' sounds *but* if the stress mark is on the α (άι) or on the ο (όι), then the two vowels are pronounced separately.
Example: νεράιδα/*nera-eedha*/fairy and ρολόι/*roloee*/watch

If the word is not stressed on the α or ο and we still want to pronounce the letters separately as 'a-ee' or 'o-ee', then we must put two little dots on the ϊ.
Example: μαϊμού/*maeemoo*/monkey and απλοϊκός/*aplo-eekos*/simple.

And finally, unlike ancient Greek where there were a lot of different stress marks, in Modern Greek there is only one. It is always on a vowel and this is the vowel that we put the emphasis on. For example, the word for good morning – καλημέρα/*kaleemera* – is stressed on the 'e', so we say καλημέρα/*kaleemera*.

We never use a stress mark on capital letters.

The Greek Alphabet

The Greek alphabet contains 24 letters. Some of the letters look and sound like in English such as Α, Ε, Ζ, Ι, Κ, Μ, Ν, Ο, Τ.

Some other letters look like their English equivalents but sound differently such as Β, Η, Ρ, Υ, Χ.

Which leaves us with some totally different letters such as Γ, Δ, Θ, Λ, Ξ, Π, Σ, Φ, Ψ, Ω.

Α α	*alfa*	Ν ν	*nee*
Β β	*veeta*	Ξ ξ	*ksee*
Γ γ	*ghama*	Ο ο	*omeekron*
Δ δ	*dhelta*	Π π	*pee*
Ε ε	*epseelon*	Ρ ρ	*ro*
Ζ ζ	*zeeta*	Σ σ ς	*seeghma*
Η η	*eeta*	Τ τ	*taf*
Θ θ	*theeta*	Υ υ	*eepseelon*
Ι ι	*yota*	Φ φ	*fee*
Κ κ	*kappa*	Χ χ	*khee*
Λ λ	*lamdha*	Ψ ψ	*psee*
Μ μ	*mee*	Ω ω	*omegha*

Χαίρω πολύ
Pleased to meet you

1

In this unit we will look at introductions: greeting one another, saying where you are from, where you live, what work you do and your nationality, and we'll also learn the first six letters of the Greek alphabet.

Traveller's tip

Greece has always been a popular holiday destination, whether for the fascination of its ancient history and mythology and its numerous archeological sites, or for the fun, adventure and sunshine of its islands; Greece has something to offer everyone. With the boom in package holidays in the 1970s and 80s the Greek islands became more popular than ever, but nowadays many people prefer to travel independently to explore the less busy or 'touristy' parts of Greece. The rise of budget tour operators and airlines and the possibility of booking internal flights, ferry crossings, trains, car hire and accommodation online have opened up parts of the country that were previously unknown to overseas tourists. Many travellers are now choosing to spend their holidays hiking in the Pindus Mountains, the principal mountain range that forms the 'backbone' of Greece, extending down through the Peloponnese and Crete, or to stay in the 'agrotourist units' being developed in many rural areas, where they can attend workshops learning local arts and crafts. It is in these unspoiled parts of Greece that you will need to put your language skills to the test as the majority of local people don't speak English and communication may become problematic. But it is also true to say that in these parts of the country you will experience the real Greek hospitality, or as we say in Greek, "Φιλοξενία".

In this unit we will learn the difference between formal and informal greetings and how to conjugate the verb 'to be'.

Listen up 1

Two neighbours, a man and a woman, meet in the street. You can follow the conversations below as you listen to them, then you'll find a series of explanations and exercises linked to them on the next few pages. 1

Mr Petridis	Γειά σας κυρία Μάνου.
Mrs Manou	Γειά σας κύριε Πετρίδη.
Mr Petridis	Τί κάνετε;
Mrs Manou	Πολύ καλά, ευχαριστώ. Εσείς;
Mr Petridis	Μιά χαρά.
Mrs Manou	Αντίο σας κύριε Πετρίδη.
Mr Petridis	Αντίο σας κυρία Μάνου, χάρηκα που σας είδα.
Mrs Manou	Και εγώ επίσης.

Two friends, Maria and Anna, meet outside a café.

Maria	Γειά σου Άννα.
Anna	Γειά σου Μαρία.
Maria	Τί κάνεις;
Anna	Μιά χαρά, εσύ;
Maria	῎Ετσι κι έτσι.
Anna	Γειά σου Μαρία, χάρηκα που σε είδα.
Maria	Και εγώ επίσης.

Words and phrases 1

Γειά σου/Γειά σας	Hello or goodbye
Τί κάνεις;/Τί κάνετε;	How are you?
Κυρία	Mrs
Κύριος/Κύριε	Mr
Ευχαριστώ	Thank you
Μιά χαρά	Fine
Πολύ καλά	Very well
Έτσι κι έτσι	So-so
Χάρηκα που σε είδα/χάρηκα που σας είδα	Nice seeing you
Και εγώ επίσης	Me too
Αντίο/Αντίο σας	Goodbye

Unlocking the language 1

In Greek, there are two ways of addressing people: formally and informally. When you are speaking to people that you don't know well, or that are older or more senior than you, you use the formal way of speaking. When you are talking to children or members of your family, or chatting with your friends, then you use the informal way.

Formal way of speaking

Γειά **σας**	Hello
Τί **κάνετε;**	How are you?
Εσείς	You
Αντίο **σας**	Goodbye
Χάρηκα που **σας** είδα	Nice seeing you

Informal way of speaking

Γειά **σου**	Hello
Τί **κάνεις;**	How are you?
Εσύ	You
Χάρηκα που **σε** είδα	Nice seeing you

Tips

- The word 'mister' is **κύριος** but when you address somebody you say **κύριε**.
- The expression '**γειά σου/γειά σας**' is used for both hello and goodbye.

Your turn 1

Fill in the gaps to check your understanding of the dialogue. You can find the answers to this and all other exercises in the answer key at www.collinslanguage.com/click. 1

– Γειά σας .... Μάνου.

– Γειά .... κύριε Πετρίδη.

– .... κάνετε;

– Πολύ ...., ευχαριστώ.................... ;

– Μιά ....

– .... σας κύριε Πετρίδη.

– Αντίο σας κυρία Μάνου, ... που σας ....

– Και εγώ ....

Find expressions in the first two dialogues to convey the following: 1

1. Hello (formal) ....
2. nice seeing you ....
3. How are you? (informal) ....
4. so-so ....
5. thank you ....
6. very well ....
7. Mr ....
8. Mrs ....

Ask Mr Smith:

How are you Mr. Smith?

Say the following in Greek:

a. Hello
b. Thank you
c. Goodbye

Listen and understand: 2

Giorgos	Γειά σου Άννα, τί κάνεις;
Anna	Μιά χαρά, εσύ;
Giorgos	Πολύ καλά.

Say whether these statements are true or false:

		True	False
1.	Giorgos is very well.	☐	☐
2.	Anna is so-so.	☐	☐

Match the Greek expressions on the left with their meaning on the right:

1. ευχαριστώ
2. κυρία
3. τί κάνεις;
4. χάρηκα που σε είδα
5. κύριε
6. αντίο
7. τί κάνετε;
8. έτσι κι έτσι

a. How are you? (informal)
b. Thank you
c. Mrs
d. How are you? (formal)
e. Mr
f. so-so
g. Nice seeing you
h. Goodbye

Pronunciation Tip

In Greek when you write in lowercase you have to put a stress mark on the vowel of the word which is stressed when pronouncing it. It is very important to stress words correctly otherwise their meanings may be different!

Listen up 2

Now listen to an informal dialogue between two young women who meet on the boat to Paros while on holiday. 3

Anna	Καλημέρα
Mirella	Καλημέρα
Anna	Πώς σε λένε;
Mirella	Με λένε Μιρέλλα. Εσένα;
Anna	Με λένε Άννα.
Mirella	Από πού είσαι;
Anna	Είμαι από την Ελλάδα, είμαι Ελληνίδα. Εσύ;
Mirella	Είμαι Ιταλίδα.
Anna	Πού μένεις Μιρέλλα;
Mirella	Μένω στο Μιλάνο. Εσύ;
Anna	Εγώ μένω στην Αθήνα. Είμαι φοιτήτρια και σπουδάζω οικονομικά.
Mirella	Εγώ δουλεύω στην τράπεζα, είμαι λογίστρια.

Listen to this formal dialogue taking place in the evening, between a man and a woman finding out more about each other: 4

Mr Smith	Καλησπέρα
Mrs Karra	Καλησπέρα σας
Mr Smith	Με λένε Πωλ Σμιθ.
Mrs Karra	Χαίρω πολύ. Με λένε Ελένη Καρρά.
Mr Smith	Από πού είσαστε κυρία Καρρά;
Mrs Karra	Είμαι Ελληνίδα. Εσείς;
Mr Smith	Είμαι Αυστραλός.
Mrs Karra	Πού μένετε;
Mr Smith	Μένω στην Μελβούρνη. Εσείς;
Mrs Karra	Μένω στην Σπάρτη.
Mr Smith	Τί δουλειά κάνετε;
Mrs Karra	Είμαι γιατρός. Εσείς;
Mr Smith	Είμαι φαρμακοποιός.

Words and phrases 2

Καλημέρα	Good morning.
Καλησπέρα	Good evening.
Πώς σε/σας λένε;	What's your name?
Με λένε...	My name is...
Από πού είσαι/είσαστε;	Where are you from?
Χαίρω πολύ	Pleased to meet you.
Πού μένεις/μένετε;	Where do you live?
φοιτήτρια *f*/φοιτητής *m*	student
Σπουδάζω οικονομικά	I study economics.
Δουλεύω στην τράπεζα	I work in the bank.
Ελληνίδα *f*/Έλληνας *m*	Greek
Ιταλίδα *f*/Ιταλός *m*	Italian
λογιστής *m*/λογίστρια *f*	accountant
γιατρός	doctor
φαρμακοποιός	pharmacist

Unlocking the language 2

The verb 'to be'

Look at the highlighted words – **είμαι** Ελληνίδα/**είμαι** λογίστρια/από πού **είσαι** – they are parts of the verb 'to be/**είμαι**'.

I am	**εγώ**/*egho*	**είμαι**/*eeme*
You are	**εσύ**/*esee*	**είσαι**/*eese*
He/she is	**αυτός, αυτή**/*aftos, aftee*	**είναι**/*eene*
We are	**εμείς**/*emees*	**είμαστε**/*eemaste*
You are	**εσείς**/*esees*	**είσαστε**/*eesaste*
They are	**αυτοί,αυτές**/*aftee, aftes m, f*	**είναι**/*eene*

Nationalities

Άγγλος *m*/**Αγγλίδα** *f*	English
Ιταλός *m*/**Ιταλίδα** *f*	Italian

Έλληνας *m*/**Ελληνίδα** *f*	Greek
Αμερικανός *m*/**Αμερικανίδα** *f*	American
Αυστραλός *m*/**Αυστραλέζα** *f*	Australian
Καναδός *m*/**Καναδέζα** *f*	Canadian
Ιρλανδός *m*/**Ιρλανδέζα** *f*	Irish
Σκωτσέζος *m*/**Σκωτσέζα** *f*	Scottish
Ουαλλός *m*/**Ουαλλέζα** *f*	Welsh

As you can see, nationalities are spelt with a capital letter and their endings vary depending on whether the person is male or female.

Learning the Greek Alphabet

Let's revise the first six letters of the Greek alphabet:

Α α	*alpha*	the letter sound is	a	as in apple
Β β	*veeta*		v	as in violin
Γ γ	*ghama*		y	as in yes
Δ δ	*dhelta*		th	as in this
Ε ε	*epseelon*		e	as in end
Ζ ζ	*zeeta*		z	as in zoo

Your turn 2

Check how much you have understood of the Listen up 2 dialogues. Refer to the Words and phrases 2 section to help you: 3

		True	**False**
1.	Mirella is Italian.	☐	☐
2.	Anna lives in Sparti.	☐	☐
3.	Mr Smith is Australian.	☐	☐
4.	Mrs Karra is a chemist.	☐	☐

Match the capital letter with its equivalent lowercase letter:

a.	Α	1.	ε
b.	Β	2.	δ
c.	Γ	3.	α
d.	Δ	4.	ζ
e.	Ε	5.	β
f.	Ζ	6.	γ

Can you say the following sentences in Greek? Check your answers by listening to the audio track. 5

1. I'm English. *f*
2. I'm Greek. *m*
3. I'm a student. *m*
4. I live in Milan.
5. I am an accountant. *f*

Listen carefully and underline the words you hear: 6

Καλημέρα	υχαριστώ	κύριος	λογίστρια	γειά σου
αντίο σας	γειά σας	κυρία	αντίο	

Fill in the gaps with words from the list below:

Έλληνας σε με Ελληνίδα δουλεύουμε δουλεύω

Καλημέρα, ... λένε Μαρία, είμαι ...., μένω στον Βόλο, ... στην τράπεζα

Let's recap

Here's an opportunity for you to revise the language you've learnt in this unit.

Supply the correct option in each case.

1. .... Ιταλίδα;

   a. Είμαι   b. Είσαι   c. Είμαστε

2. Ναι, ... Ιταλίδα.

   a. είμαστε   b. είμαι   c. είναι

3. .... φοιτητής. Σπουδάζω οικονομικά.

   a. Είμαι   b. Είμαστε   c. Είναι

4. Η Άννα .... από την Αθήνα.

   a. είσαι   b. είμαι   c. είναι

Write the feminine nationality next to the masculine one:

1. Έλληνας ....
2. Ιταλός ....
3. Αμερικανός ....
4. Άγγλος ....
5. Ιρλανδός ....
6. Καναδός ....

Match the start of the sentence on the left with the end of the sentence on the right:

1. Ο Γιώργος	a. είναι Άγγλος
2. Η Χριστίνα	b. είναι λογιστής
3. Ο κύριος Ιωάννου	c. είναι φοιτητής
4. Η Έλεν	d. είναι φοιτήτρια
5. Ο Πώλ	e. είναι Ιρλανδέζα

Κουβεντιάζοντας
Talking to people

In this unit we will be talking about family and friends. We will learn vocabulary about family members, numbers up to 20 and look at the next six letters of the Greek alphabet. We will also learn the definite and indefinite articles, and about nouns and their different gender endings.

Traveller's tip

In Greece, there is always an excuse to celebrate. In addition to the major religious events such as Christmas, New Year, Easter etc. Greek people celebrate weddings, christenings, birthdays and name days. But what is a name day? In the Greek Orthdox calendar every day of the year is dedicated to a saint. If you happen to share the same name, then you celebrate your name day on that day. For example, the 6th of December is Saint Nicholas' Day. On name days people ring you to wish you many happy returns and you may invite them to your house for a drink or for a meal. In the past, name days meant having a party which was open to everyone but nowadays it is by invitation only.

Churches also commemorate their saint's special day by organising a festival with free food and live traditional music and many remote chapels will only open on their saint's name day. Many of the Greek islands and villages have patron saints. For example, in Corfu (Kerkyra) the patron saint is Agios Spydidon and in Zante (Zakynthos) the patron saint is Agios Dionisios.

In Greek families it is traditional for the eldest son to be named after the grandfather, usually the paternal grandfather, and the eldest daughter named after the grandmother.

In this unit we will be working with articles and gender and we will also introduce some regular verbs, learn numbers up to 20 and look at the next six letters of the Greek alphabet.

Listen up 1

Eleni invites her new friend Ann to her house to meet her family. You can follow their conversation below as you listen. Listen to the dialogue as many times as you need to and then fill in the gaps in Your turn 1 to check your understanding. 7

Eleni	Να σου συστήσω τους γονείς μου. Ο πατέρας μου και η μητέρα μου.
Ann	Χαίρω πολύ. Με λένε Αννν.
Eleni	Αυτός είναι ο αδελφός μου, ο Γιάννης και αυτή είναι η αδελφή μου, η Χριστίνα.
Ann	Χαίρω πολύ, έχω και εγώ έναν αδελφό.
Eleni	Πόσο χρονών είναι ο αδελφός σου;
Ann	Ο Μάρκ είναι δεκαπέντε χρονών.

Words and phrases 1

Να σου συστήσω...	Let me introduce you to...
οι γονείς	... the parents
ο πατέρας	... the father
η μητέρα	... the mother
ο αδελφός	... the brother
η αδελφή	... the sister
αυτός	this *m*
αυτή	this *f*

Unlocking the language 1

Greek nouns are usually preceded either by the definite article 'the' or the indefinite article 'a'. Unlike English, in Greek there are three genders: masculine, feminine and neuter. The definite article is **ο** for the masculine, **η** for the feminine, and **το** for the neuter. The indefinite article is **ένας** for the masculine, **μία** for the feminine, and **ένα** for the neuter. Here are some examples of masculine, feminine and neuter words:

Masculine	**Feminine**	**Neuter**
ο/ένας αδελφός (brother)	**η/μία αδελφή** (sister)	**το/ένα παιδί** (child)
ο/ένας πατέρας (father)	**η/μία μητέρα** (mother)	**το/ένα αγόρι** (boy)
ο/ένας άντρας (husband)	**η/μία γυναίκα** (wife)	**το/ένα μωρό** (baby)
ο/ένας φίλος (boyfriend)	**η/μία φίλη/φιλενάδα** (girlfriend)	

The words **φίλος /φίλη** ('boyfriend/girlfriend') are also used for 'friend'.

'Partner in life' is **σύντροφος** but a 'business partner' is **συνέταιρος.**

Tip

There are no rules as to which nouns are masculine, feminine or neuter but most of the time you can guess the gender by the noun's ending. Look closely at the examples above. What do you notice?

Masculine nouns end in **-ς**
Feminine nouns end in **-η** and **-α**
Neuter nouns end in **-ι** and **-ο**

Your turn 1

Fill in the gaps to check your understanding: 7

Eleni: Να σου .... τους γονείς μου. Ο.................... μου και η μητέρα μου.

Ann: .... πολύ. Με λένε Ανν.

Eleni: Αυτός είναι ο .... μου, ο Γιάννης και αυτή είναι η .... μου, η Χριστίνα.

Ann: Χαίρω ...., έχω και εγώ έναν αδελφό.

Eleni: Πόσο .... είναι ο αδελφός σου;

Ann: Ο Μάρκ είναι .... χρονών.

Find expressions in the dialogue to convey the following: 7

1. Pleased to meet you. ....
2. This is my sister. ....
3. How old is your brother? ....
4. Let me introduce you to my parents. ....

Pronunciation Tip

The combination '**αι**' in the words **χαίρω** and **και** sounds like an '**ε**'.

In the same way, the combination '**ει**' in **θεία** and **είναι** sounds like an '**ι**'.

Say the following in Greek: 8

a. This is my mother
b. How old is your sister?
c. This is my brother.
d. Sally, let me introduce my brother to you.

Listen carefully and circle the words you hear. Check your answers by listening to the audio track. 9

Χαίρω πολύ αδελφός μητέρα πατέρας αδελφή γονείς

Select the appropriate definite article to put in front of each noun. You can check all your answers online at www.collinslanguage.com/click.

το η το ο η το ο

1. .... αδελφός
2. .... αγόρι
3. .... μητέρα
4. .... αδελφή
5. .... μωρό
6. .... πατέρας
7. .... παιδί

Listen up 2

Later on the same evening Eleni and Ann go to a café where they meet Eleni's cousin. You can follow the conversation below as you listen to it. Then you can check your understanding in Your turn 2. Refer to the Words and phrases 2 section if you need more explanations. 10

Eleni	Να σου συστήσω τον ξάδερφο μου, τον Κώστα.
Ann	Χαίρω πολύ.
Eleni	Ο Κώστας είναι ο γυιός του θείου και της θείας μου.
Ann	Πόσο χρονών είσαι Κώστα;
Kostas	Είμαι είκοσι χρονών. Εσύ;
Ann	Εγώ είμαι δεκαοκτώ χρονών.
Eleni	Εσύ έχεις ξαδέρφια;
Ann	Ναι, έχω μία ξαδέρφη, την Σάλλυ. Η Σάλλυ είναι παντρεμένη και έχει μία κόρη και ένα γυιό.

Words and phrases 2

Πόσο χρονών είσαι;	How old are you?
ο ξάδερφος	cousin *m*
η ξαδέρφη	cousin *f*
ο γυιός	son
η κόρη	daughter
παντρεμένη	married *f*
ο θείος	uncle
η θεία	aunt

Unlocking the language 2

The verb 'to have'

Here is how to conjugate the verb 'to have/**έχω**' in the present tense. A lot of verbs have the same conjugation in the present tense, such as 'to work/**δουλεύω**', 'to study/**σπουδάζω**', 'to stay/live/**μένω**'.

Εγώ	έχω
Εσύ	έχεις
Αυτός, αυτή, αυτό	έχει
Εμείς	έχουμε
Εσείς	έχετε
Αυτοί, αυτές, αυτά	έχουν

Tip

In Greek, you don't need to put I, you, he or she, etc. in front of the verb. You just conjugate the verb on its own. The only time you put the personal pronouns in front of the verb is when you want to emphasise who did what.

Numbers

1	ένα	**11**	έντεκα
2	δύο	**12**	δώδεκα
3	τρία	**13**	δεκατρία
4	τέσσερα	**14**	δεκατέσσερα
5	πέντε	**15**	δεκαπέντε
6	έξι	**16**	δεκαέξι
7	επτά	**17**	δεκαεπτά
8	οκτώ	**18**	δεκαοκτώ
9	εννέα	**19**	δεκαεννέα
10	δέκα	**20**	είκοσι

Numbers above twelve are very straightforward to form. You just put the tens and the units together. For example, for 13 you say **δεκατρία**, for 24 you say **εικοσιτέσσερα**.

Learning the Greek alphabet

Now let's revise the next six letters of the Greek alphabet.

Η η	*eeta*	the letter sound is	i	as in ink
Θ θ	*theeta*		th	as in theatre
Ι ι	*gheeota*		i	as in ink
Κ κ	*kapa*		k	as in key
Λ λ	*lamdha*		l	as in lake
Μ μ	*mee*		m	as in man

Your turn 2

Check your understanding of the dialogue. True or false? 10

		True	False
1.	Kostas is eighteen years old.	☐	☐
2.	Eleni and Kostas are cousins.	☐	☐
3.	Sally's cousin is married.	☐	☐
4.	She has two sons.	☐	☐

Match the words with the figures:

a.	1	1.	τρία
b.	5	2.	έξι
c.	3	3.	δεκαοκτώ
d.	12	4.	ένα
e.	8	5.	δεκαπέντε
f.	6	6.	πέντε
g.	15	7.	οκτώ
h.	18	8.	δώδεκα

Listen carefully and then tick the correct boxes: 11

Eleni	Μαρία, να σου συστήσω το ξάδερφό μου τον Γιάννη. Είναι δεκαεννέα χρονών.

	True	False
5. Eleni is introducing her brother Yannis to Maria.	☐	☐
6. Yannis is eighteen years old.	☐	☐

Now you are going to listen to the Greek numbers 1 to 20. Listen carefully to track 12 and try counting from 1 to 20 yourself. 12

ένα δύο τρία τέσσερα πέντε

έξι επτά οκτώ εννέα δέκα

έντεκα δώδεκα δεκατρία δεκατέσσερα δεκαπέντε

δεκαέξι δεκαεπτά δεκαοκτώ δεκαεννέα είκοσι

Match the words written in capitals with the appropriate ones written in lowercase:

1. ΘΕΙΑ — a. γη
2. ΓΑΛΑ — b. θέα
3. ΚΛΙΜΑ — c. μέλι
4. ΒΕΛΗ — d. δέμα
5. ΓΗ — e. γάλα
6. ΘΕΑ — f. θεία
7. ΔΕΜΑ — g. βέλη
8. ΜΕΛΙ — h. κλίμα

Let's recap

Match the masculine relative with the appropriate feminine one:

1. αδελφός	a. κόρη
2. θείος	b. ξαδέρφη
3. πατέρας	c. αδελφή
4. γυιός	d. μητέρα
5. ξάδερφος	e. θεία

Complete the sentences with the appropriate form of the verbs:

1. Η Μαρία .... μία αδελφή.
   a. έχω b. έχετε c. έχει d. έχουμε
2. Ο Γιάννης και η Άννα .... στην Αθήνα.
   a. μένουν b. μένω c. μένει d. μένεις
3. Ελένη, πού .... ;
   a. μένουμε b. μένετε c. μένεις d. μένει
4. Ο Κώστας .... στην τράπεζα.
   a. δουλεύει b. δουλεύεις c. δουλεύετε d. δουλεύουμε

Στο ξενοδοχείο
At the hotel

3

In this unit we will cover the language you'll need to check into a hotel in Greece and ask about what facilities it has. We'll also be taking a look at some of the different types of places you can stay in Greece.

Traveller's tip

Every year millions of tourists head off to Greece in search of sunshine, good food and drink, culture and the ultimate in relaxation.

Naturally enough, most hotels and tourism staff speak some English. However, there's a great sense of achievement in using some basic Greek on holiday, and Greeks will be delighted that you've made an effort to learn their language.

Your first experience of a Greek hotel is likely to be on one of Greece's coasts or islands, usually as part of a package holiday. But once the travel bug has bitten you, you may want to do things more independently. Here are a few of the key words to look out for in considering where to stay.

If you are on a modest budget, **Ενοικιαζόμενα δωμάτια** might provide the type of accommodation you're looking for. These are usually family-run independent rooms with a private shower.

Facilities tend to be very basic, and generally they don't serve breakfast or accept credit cards.

You can also find **Ενοικιαζόμενες γκαρσονιέρες**, which are self-catering studios equipped with a small kitchen.

Another type of accommodation is **Παραδοσιακοί ξενώνες**, which are rooms in a house which has been restored in the region's traditional style and at a very high standard. They may be either independent self-catering studios or part of the main house, a bit like a Bed & Breakfast.

Backpackers should also look for **κάμπινγ**, an organised campsite.

In this unit we will learn the days of the week, the months and the numbers 30 to 100. We will also learn how to ask questions and review the next set of letters in the Greek alphabet.

Listen up 1

13

Peter wants to book his holiday for next summer and he phones his favourite hotel in Greece. From now on you will not see the transcript here in the book but you can always go online to access all of the transcripts at www.collinslanguage.com/click.

Tip

Κλείνω means 'to close' but it is also used for the following expressions: 'to book' and 'to seal':
I would like to book **θέλω να κλείσω**
seal a deal **κλείνω μια συμφωνία**

Words and phrases 1

το δωμάτιο		room
ένα (δωμάτιο)	μονόκλινο	single room
	δίκλινο	double room
	δίκλινο με διπλό κρεβάτι	with a double bed
	δίκλινο με δύο μονά κρεβάτια	with two single beds (twin)
	με μπάνιο	with a bathroom
	με ντούς	with a shower
Θα το πάρω		I will take it
Η προκαταβολή		the deposit

Unlocking the language 1

Numbers from 30 to 100

30	**τριάντα**
31	**τριάντα ένα**
32	**τριάντα δύο**
40	**σαράντα**
46	**σαράντα έξι**
50	**πενήντα**
60	**εξήντα**
70	**εβδομήντα**
80	**ογδόντα**
90	**ενενήντα**
100	**εκατό**

Days of the week

In Greek, all the days of the week are feminine nouns except for Saturday.

Monday	**Δευτέρα**	Friday	**Παρασκευή**
Tuesday	**Τρίτη**	Saturday	**Σάββατο**
Wednesday	**Τετάρτη**	Sunday	**Κυριακή**
Thursday	**Πέμπτη**		

If you want to say 'on Monday' or 'on Tuesday', etc. you say **την Δευτέρα, την Τρίτη** and if you want to say 'from ... to', you say **από την Δευτέρα μέχρι την Τρίτη**.

Your turn 1

Check your understanding. True or false?

13

		True	False
1.	Peter wants to book a single room with a shower.	☐	☐
2.	He wants to stay five days.	☐	☐
3.	The room costs ninety-five euros per night.	☐	☐

Find expressions in Listen up 1 to convey the following: 13

1. I would like to book a room.
2. for five days
3. of course
4. from Monday till Saturday
5. How much does it cost?
6. Can you send a deposit?

How do you say the following expressions in Greek? Listen to the audio track to check your answers. 14

1. a single room with a shower
2. a double room with a bathroom
3. a twin room
4. a room with a double bed
5. a room for 10 days

Listen carefully to Track 15 and circle the numbers you hear. 15

30	32	38	42	45	56	57	60
62	71	74	81	85	92	96	

Listen up 2

A young tourist couple arrive at their hotel reception ready to check-in. Listen to the dialogue. You can use the Words and phrases 2 section to check some of the dialogue you'll hear in this track. 16

Words and phrases 2

Έχουμε κλείσει ...	We have booked ...
Καλώς ορίσατε	Welcome
Προτιμώ	I prefer
ασανσέρ	lift
όροφος	floor
δεύτερο	second
ισόγειο	the ground floor
Περιλαμβάνει Το πρωϊνό;	Is breakfast included?
η πισίνα	the swimming pool
το εστιατόριο	the restaurant
το γυμναστήριο	the gym
Ορίστε.	Here you are.
κλειδί	key
Καλή διαμονή.	Have a nice stay.

Unlocking the language 2

Asking questions

You can turn a sentence into a question just by adding a question mark at the end of your sentence and changing the tone of your voice. For example, the verb **υπάρχει** means 'there is', but with the question mark – a semi-colon in Greek, **υπάρχει**; – at the end it means 'is there?' Here are some useful words to help you with asking questions:

Where	**πού**
When	**πότε**
How	**πώς**
What	**τί**
From where	**από πού**
What for	**για τί**
How much	**πόσο**

Months of the year

In Greek, months are masculine nouns and they all end in -s.

January	**Ιανουάριος**
February	**Φεβρουάριος**
March	**Μάρτιος**
April	**Απρίλιος**
May	**Μάιος**
June	**Ιούνιος**
July	**Ιούλιος**
August	**Αύγουστος**
September	**Σεπτέμβριος**
October	**Οκτώβριος**
November	**Νοέμβριος**
December	**Δεκέμβριος**

Tips

If you want to say 'in January', 'in February', etc. you must drop the final -s and add the masculine article **τον**. So you will say: **τον Ιανουάριο**, **τον Φεβρουάριο**.

On the other hand, if you want to say 'on the 2nd of March' or 'on the 5th of April', then you change the ending by dropping the -s and replacing it with '**υ**'. The sound then changes to 'oo'. So you say: 2 **Μαρτίου**, **5 Απριλίου**.

Some more alphabet revision

Now let's look at the next set of letters in the Greek alphabet:

Ν ν	*nee*	the letter sound is	n	as in knee
Ξ ξ	*ksee*		x	as in ox
Ο ο	*omeekron*		o	as in orange
Π π	*pee*		p	as in peace
Ρ ρ	*ro*		r	as in read
Σ σς	*seeghma*		s	as in set

Tip

When a word contains an -s you should use -**σ** if it is in the beginning or the middle of the word and -**ς** if it is at the end of the word. For example: **στάση**, **Μάρτιος**

Your turn 2

Check your understanding of the dialogue by completing the sentence with the missing words: 16

Έχουμε ένα δωμάτιο με.................. κρεβάτι στον .... όροφο και ένα .... με δύο.................. κρεβάτια στο ....

Match the questions in the left-hand column with the correct answer on the right:

1. Μου δίνετε ένα διαβατήριο παρακαλώ;
2. Πόσο κάνει το δωμάτιο;
3. Πού είναι το εστιατόριο;
4. Περιλαμβάνει και το πρωϊνό;

a. Στο ισόγειο
b. Ορίστε
c. Όχι, το πρωϊνό κάνει 5 ευρώ
d. 45 ευρώ

Listen carefully to track 17 and choose the correct option to complete each sentence: 17

1. Εχουμε κλείσει ένα .... γιά πέντε μέρες.
   - κάμπινγκ
   - ξενοδοχείο
   - ξενώνα
   - δωμάτιο
2. Το δωμάτιο σας είναι .... δεύτερο όροφο.
   - στήν
   - στον
   - στούς
   - στα
3. .... ασανσέρ στο ξενοδοχείο;
   - Υπάρχω
   - Υπάρχει
   - Υπάρχετε
   - Υπάρχουμε
4. Ορίστε το κλειδί σας, ... διαμονή!
   - καλά
   - καλός
   - καλό
   - καλή

Can you say the following days of the week in Greek? You can listen to track 18 to check whether you've got them right. 18

Monday Tuesday Friday Sunday Thursday

Now try to say the following months in Greek, then listen to track 19 to check whether you've got them right. 19

January April July November May

Match the words written in capitals with the words written in lowercase letters:

a.	ΒΙΒΛΙΟ	1.	πόδι
b.	ΚΟΡΗ	2.	ξένος
c.	ΛΕΞΗ	3.	ρόδινο
d.	ΚΛΕΙΔΙ	4.	βιβλίο
e.	ΞΕΝΟΣ	5.	κόρη
f.	ΠΙΑΝΟ	6.	λέξη
g.	ΠΟΔΙ	7.	κλειδί
h.	ΡΟΔΙΝΟ	8.	πιάνο

Let's recap

Choose from the options below to complete the questions:

Πόσο Πού Από πού Τί

1. .... δωμάτιο θέλετε;
   Ένα δίκλινο με μπάνιο.
2. .... κάνει;
   45 ευρώ.
3. .... είσαστε;
   Από την Αθήνα.
4. .... είναι το εστιατόριο;
   Είναι στο ισόγειο.

Put the words below in alphabetical order:

1.	μονόκλινο	a.	....
2.	ασανσέρ	b.	....
3.	δίκλινο	c.	....
4.	γυμναστήριο	d.	....
5.	πισίνα	e.	....
6.	διαβατήριο	f.	....
7.	προκαταβολή	g.	....
8.	εστιατόριο	h.	....

4 Πού είναι ...; Where is ...?

This unit is all about directions and travelling and contains useful vocabulary for buying tickets and asking prices and times.

Traveller's tip

Athens is a lively city that never sleeps. It is a city rich in history, with lots of museums and archeological sites to visit. A good place to start exploring is Syntagma Square. At the top of the Square is the Parliament building and, next to that, the National Garden. At the bottom of the Square is Ermou Street, a shopper's paradise, which leads to Monastiraki and Plaka, where you can buy your souvenirs and eat in one of the numerous tavernas. From Plaka, continue your stroll towards the Acropolis and Thission and visit the newly opened Acropolis Museum.

If you visit some of the Metro stations you will see the antiquities that were found during the excavations as well as paintings and sculptures by famous Greek artists such as Fassianos, Mytaras, Gaitis, Varotsos and Moralis. Or, if you prefer, you can take the tram and go south of Athens to the sea at Faliron, Kalamaki or Glyfada, where there are good beaches for swimming, trendy cafés and restaurants and beautiful marinas.

Public transport is very efficient in Athens. In addition to the buses, there is the Metro, trams and the trolley bus. Or you can opt for a taxi. Taxis in Athens are yellow and their fares are very reasonable.

Travelling in Greece is easy. You can either book your ferry or flights online, or pop into a travel agent to buy your tickets there.

In this unit we will practise ordinal numbers and time. We will also practise the last six letters of the Greek alphabet.

Listen up 1

Peter is visiting Athens and would like to take the Metro to the city centre. He stops a passer-by and asks for directions.

20

Words and phrases 1

συγνώμη	excuse me
ο σταθμός	the station
θα πάτε ίσια	you will go straight on
θα περάσετε	you will pass
τα φανάρια	the traffic lights
το στενό	the little narrow street
αριστερά	left
δεξιά	right
δεύτερος	second

Unlocking the language 1

Have you noticed the word **δεύτερο**? It means 'second'. In Greek, ordinal numbers are like adjectives. They agree in number, gender and case with the noun they are referring to. For example, in the dialogue, **στενό** is neuter. If you had a masculine word, such as road/**δρόμος**, the ordinal number would be **δεύτερος** but a feminine word, such as street/**οδός**, would be **δεύτερη**. Let's look at the ordinal numbers from first to tenth.

1st	**πρώτος**	**πρώτη**	**πρώτο**
2nd	**δεύτερος**	**δεύτερη**	**δεύτερο**

3rd	**τρίτος**	**τρίτη**	**τρίτο**
4th	**τέταρτος**	**τέταρτη**	**τέταρτο**
5th	**πέμπτος**	**πέμπτη**	**πέμπτο**
6th	**έκτος**	**έκτη**	**έκτο**
7th	**έβδομος**	**έβδομη**	**έβδομο**
8th	**όγδοος**	**όγδοη**	**όγδοο**
9th	**ένατος**	**ένατη**	**ένατο**
10th	**δέκατος**	**δέκατη**	**δέκατο**

Your turn 1

Check your understanding of the dialogue. True or false? 20

		True	False
1.	The passer-by is looking for the bus stop.	☐	☐
2.	It is before the traffic lights.	☐	☐
3.	It's a 100 metres away.	☐	☐

Find in the dialogue expressions which convey the following: 20

1. Where is the Metro station?
2. You will go straight on.
3. You will pass the traffic lights.
4. You will turn left at the second little street.
5. The station is on the right.
6. Is it far?

Pronunciation Tip

The combination letters '**ευ**'and '**αυ**' are pronounced in two ways. Sometimes they sound as 'ef' or 'af', as in **ευχαριστώ**/thank you, and sometimes as 'ev' or 'av',, as in **ευγενικό**/polite.

Can you say the following words in Greek? 21

1. excuse me
2. the station
3. the traffic lights
4. second
5. right
6. left
7. far
8. 100 metres

Listen to the short dialogue and tick the appropriate boxes: 22

		True	False
1.	Peter has to turn at the third street on the left.	☐	☐
2.	The bank is on the left.	☐	☐

Match the ordinal numbers on the left with the cardinal numbers on the right:

a.	τρίτος	1.	ένα
b.	πέμπτος	2.	τέσσερα
c.	δεύτερος	3.	δέκα
d.	έκτος	4.	τρία
e.	όγδοος	5.	πέντε
f.	δέκατος	6.	έξι
g.	πρώτος	7.	δύο
h.	τέταρτος	8.	οκτώ

Listen up 2

Mary is at a travel agent's booking a ferry ticket to go to Poros. Poros is a beautiful little island just an hour's journey on the Flying Dolphin from Piraeus – an ideal destination for a day trip. Listen to the dialogue and then use the Words and phrases 2 section to help you practise booking your own tickets.

23

Words and phrases 2

Κάθε πότε έχει καράβι ...;	How often is there a boat for ...?
κάθε μέρα	every day
το πρωί	morning
το μεσημέρι	midday
το απόγευμα	afternoon
Θα ήθελα ένα εισιτήριο.	I would like a ticket.
Γιά πότε;	For when?
οκτώ και τέταρτο	8:15
δύο και μισή	2:30
Απλό ή με επιστροφή;	Single or return?
Καλό Ταξίδι.	Have a safe journey.

Unlocking the language 2

Telling the time

To ask the time in Greek you say **Τί ώρα είναι**. One important thing to remember is that the time goes first, followed by **και** for past the hour or **παρά** for to the hour. For example: 2:05 will be **δύο και πέντε** and 4:50 will be **πέντε παρά δέκα**. In Greece, people mainly use the 12-hour clock and **πμ** for am and **μμ** for pm. One more thing to remember is that the hour is feminine and therefore for 'one', 'three' and 'four', you say **μία, τρεις, τέσσερις**. To say 'half past', you say **και μισή** and the word for 'quarter' is **τέταρτο**.

Learning the Greek alphabet

Ττ	*taf*	the letter sound is	t	as in tea
Υυ	*eepseelon*		i	as in ink
Φφ	*fee*		f	as in fish
Χχ	*khee*		h	as in house
Ψψ	*psee*		ps	as in cups
Ωω	*omegha*		o	as in old

Your turn 2

Check your understanding. True or false? 23

		True	False
1.	Mary wants to go to Paros.	☐	☐
2.	She wants a return ticket for Tuesday.	☐	☐
3.	The ticket costs seventeeen euros.	☐	☐

Draw lines to match the times to the appropriate clocks:

1. δύο και μισή
2. εννέα και πέντε
3. μία και τέταρτο
4. έντεκα και είκοσιπέντε
5. οκτώ παρά τέταρτο
6. έξι και είκοσι
7. πέντε παρά τέταρτο
8. δέκα και δέκα

a.

b.

c.

d.

e.

f.

g.

h.

How would you say the following expressions in Greek? (CD 24)

1. How often is there a boat to Paros?
2. I would like a return ticket.
3. for Saturday
4. Have a safe journey.
5. 5:20
6. 9:30

Listen to the dialogue and say whether the following are true or false: (CD 25)

		True	False
1.	There is a boat every day.	☐	☐
2.	The passenger wants a return ticket for Thursday.	☐	☐
3.	The ticket costs 56 euros.	☐	☐

Match the words written in capitals with those written in lowercase:

1.	ΜΕΣΗΜΕΡΙ	a.	απόγευμα
2.	ΩΡΑ	b.	καράβι
3.	ΕΙΣΙΤΗΡΙΟ	c.	μεσημέρι
4.	ΕΠΙΣΤΡΟΦΗ	d.	ώρα
5.	ΑΠΟΓΕΥΜΑ	e.	εισιτήριο
6.	ΚΑΡΑΒΙ	f.	επιστροφή

Let's recap

Complete the dialogue with the correct words:

- Καλημέρα, κάθε πότε έχει .... γιά την Σάμο;

  a. καρέκλα **b.** καρότσι **c.** καράβι **d.** καπέλο

- Κάθε .... στις οκτώ το πρωί.

  a. ώρα **b.** μέρα **c.** μήνα **d.** μεσημέρι

- Θα ήθελα ένα .... με επιστροφή.

  a. εισιτήριο **b.** διαβατήριο **c.** καράβι **d.** απόγευμα

- Βεβαίως.

- .... κάνει;

  a. Τί **b.** Πώς **c.** Πότε **d.** Πόσο

- 15 ευρώ.

Put the following words in alphabetical order:

ταξίδι	1.	....
καράβι	2.	....
επίστροφή	3.	....
εισιτήριο	4.	....
απλό	5.	....
μέρα	6.	....

Match the start of the sentence on the left with the end of it on the right:

1.	Τί ώρα φεύγει	a.	στίς 8:00 το πρωί
2.	Πού είναι	b.	με επιστρόφή, παρακαλώ
3.	Πόσο κάνει	c.	το καράβι;
4.	Ένα είσιτήριο	d.	ο σταθμός παρακαλώ;
5.	Κάθε μέρα	e.	το τρίτο στενό δεξιά
6.	Θα πάρετε	f.	το εισιτήριο;

Στο καφενείο
At the café

5

In this unit we will be focusing on ordering drinks and snacks at a café or as the Greeks call it: **καφενείο**.

Traveller's tip

Greeks don't have a big breakfast in the morning. Normally, they drink a Greek coffee with a koulouraki – a type of biscuit – or a glass of milk before setting off for work or school. Sometimes if they are in a hurry they might buy their coffee on the way to work, together with a spinach pie or a cheese pie or even a toasted sandwich.

Cafés are very popular in Greece. The traditional café is called a 'kafenio'. It is a place where retired men gather to drink their coffee, play backgammon or cards and talk politics. Every village has at least one kafenio, usually in the main square. In addition to Greek coffee, in a kafenio you can drink brandy, beer, soft drinks, and of course raki and ouzo. Ouzo is normally served with meze, a selection of fresh bread, feta cheese, tomatoes and a few olives.

Younger Greeks might prefer to go to a café rather than a kafenio because cafés tend to serve a greater variety of coffees and snacks and they also serve cocktails and other alcoholic drinks, but more so because a particular café is trendy.

Some more information about Greek coffee:

Greek coffee - otherwise known as Turkish or Armenian coffee - is prepared one at a time in a 'briki'. You add the right amount of water, coffee and sugar and boil it over low heat. You can have your coffee without sugar - **σκέτο**, sweet - **γλυκό**, medium - **μέτριο**, strong and sweet - **βαρύ γλυκό** or medium and weak - **ελαφρύ μέτριο** - but you must specify this when you order your coffee as all the ingredients are added and boiled together.

In this unit we will be using two expressions when asking for things: **θα ήθελα** and **μήπως έχετε**. We will also be using **δεν** to express that you don't want something or that you don't have something.

Listen up 1

Yannis and Maria are visiting a café. Listen to their conversation. 26

Words and phrases 1

ο κατάλογος	the menu
Τί θα πάρετε;	What will you have?
ο καφές	coffee
η τυρόπιτα	cheese pie
Θέλετε τίποτε άλλο;	Would you like anything else?
δυστυχώς	unfortunately
το παγωτό	ice cream
η φράουλα	strawberry
η βανίλια	vanilla
η σοκολάτα	chocolate
το φυστίκι	pistachio

Unlocking the language 1

In Greek, if you want to turn a sentence into its negative, you just add the little word **δεν** in front of the verb: **Δεν θέλω ένα παγωτό φράουλα, θέλω ένα παγωτό σοκολάτα** I don't want a strawberry ice cream, I want a chocolate ice cream.

The words 'nothing' **τίποτα**, 'never' **ποτέ** and 'nobody' **κανένας** can be added after the verb. For example: I don't want anything **δεν θέλω τίποτα.**

Your turn 1

Check your understanding of the dialogue. True or false? 26

		True	False
1.	Yannis wants a Greek coffee.	☐	☐
2.	He also wants a sandwich.	☐	☐
3.	Maria wants a chocolate ice cream.	☐	☐

Find expressions in the dialogue to convey the following: 26

1. a menu, please
2. Have you got any sandwiches?
3. a medium Greek coffee
4. unfortunately, we don't have ...
5. a chocolate ice cream
6. a cheese pie
7. straightaway
8. Here you are.

Pronunciation Tip

In Greek there are five different ways to spell the 'ι' sound: **ι**, **η**, **υ**, **οι**, **ει**

Say the following in Greek: 27

1. a menu, please
2. a cheese pie
3. a coffee
4. a vanilla ice cream
5. Have you got any sandwiches?
6. How much do they cost?

Listen to the dialogue and say whether the following statements are true or false: 28

	True	False
1. The customer wants a Greek coffee and a vanilla ice cream.	☐	☐
2. They don't have vanilla ice cream.	☐	☐
3. The customer chooses a pistachio ice cream instead.	☐	☐

Put the words in the correct order to create a full sentence:

1. καφέ θα μέτριο έναν ήθελα ελληνικό ....
2. βανίλια έχετε παγωτό μήπως; ....
3. άλλο τίποτα θέλετε; ....
4. έχουμε δυστυχώς δεν ....

Listen up 2

This time, Giorgos and Helen are ordering food and drink in a café. Listen to the dialogue as many times as you need. Further information and exercises follow on the next few pages. 29

Words and phrases 2

τοστ με ζαμπόν	toasted ham sandwich
το τυρί	cheese
η ντομάτα	tomato
η μπύρα	beer
το ποτήρι	glass
η σπανακόπιτα	spinach pie
έναν φραπέ μέτριο με γάλα	a medium iced coffee with milk
ένα μπουκάλι νερό	a bottle of water
τα ρέστα	change

Unlocking the language 2

When asking 'how much' you say **πόσο κάνει;** if you are asking the price of one item, or **πόσο κάνουν;** if you are asking the price of two or more. **Κάνει** and **κάνουν** are both parts of the verb **κάνω** that you have already seen in Unit 1.

Here are some examples of asking for just one item:

Πόσο κάνει το παγωτό;
Πόσο κάνει ο καφές;

and for more than one item:

Πόσο κάνουν ο καφές και το παγωτό;
Πόσο κάνουν η μπύρα και το νερό;

Your turn 2

Check your understanding. Fill in the gaps using the words from the dialogue:

Ορίστε, ένα .... και μία .... γιά τον κύριο και η .... και ο φραπέ γιά την κυρία και ένα .... νερό.

Match the item with the picture:

1. ένας ελληνικός καφές
2. ένα μπουκάλι νερό
3. ένα ποτήρι μπύρα
4. ένα τοστ με ζαμπόν και τυρί
5. ένας φραπέ
6. ένα παγωτό

a.

b.

c.

d.

e.

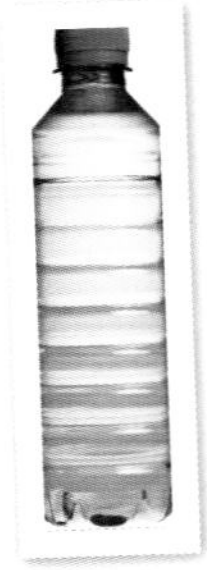

f.

Be negative! How do you say the following in Greek? 30

1. We don't have any sandwiches.
2. I don't want a Greek coffee, I want a beer.
3. Unfortunately, we don't have chocolate ice cream.
4. I don't want an iced coffee, I want a medium Greek coffee.

Listen to the dialogue and select the pictures of the items you hear being ordered. 31

a.

b.

c.

d.

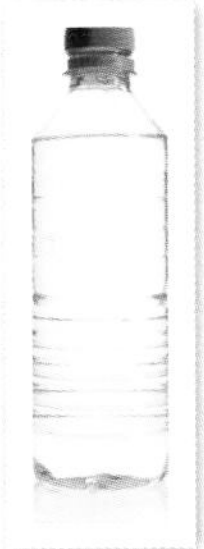

e.

f.

Unscramble these anagrams to identify the words in the box:

iced coffee	water	beer	spinach pie	bottle	change

1. ΣΑΡΤΕ...
2. ΠΑΡΕΦ...
3. ΛΜΟΠΥΙΚΑ...
4. ΟΡΕΝ...
5. ΠΑΜΥΡ...
6. ΚΣΑΝΟΠΑΙΤΑΠ...

Let's recap

Select the appropriate article to complete the sentences. Check your answers by listening to the audio track. 32

ένα	μία	έναν	ένα	μία	έναν

- ....κατάλογο παρακαλώ.
- Θα ήθελα....................παγωτό φράουλα.
- Θέλετε τίποτε άλλο;
- Ναι,....................φραπέ,....................τυρόπιττα και.................... σπανακόπιτα
- Αμέσως.
- Και....................μπουκάλι νέρο, παρακαλώ
- Βεβαίως.

Fill in the missing words to complete the dialogue. Check your answers by listening to the audio track. 33

ρέστα	ευρώ	τίποτε	κατάλογο	πάρετε	μπουκάλι	κάνουν	ούζο

- Καλημέρα, έναν .... παρακαλώ.
- Ορίστε. Τί θα .... ;
- Θα ήθελα ένα .... με μεζέ
- Θέλετε .... άλλο;
- Ένα .... νερό.

- Αμέσως.
- Πόσο .... ;
- 15 ....
- Ορίστε 20.
- Ορίστε τα .... σας.
- Ευχαριστώ.

Match the start of the sentence on the left with the end of it on the right:

1. έναν ελληνικό
2. ένα μπουκάλι
3. δύο
4. μήπως έχετε
5. έναν φραπέ
6. ένα παγωτό
7. ένα ποτήρι
8. ένα σάντουιτς

a μπύρες
b με τυρί και ντομάτα
c. κρασί
d. μέτριο
e. βανίλια
f. νερό
g. με γάλα
h. σπανακόπιττα;

Write the following words in lowercase letters. Don't forget to stress the correct letters:

1. Ο ΚΑΦΕΣ..
2. ΤΟ ΠΑΓΩΤΟ..
3. Η ΜΠΥΡΑ..
4. ΤΟ ΟΥΖΟ..
5. Η ΤΥΡΟΠΙΤΤΑ..
6. Ο ΚΑΤΑΛΟΓΟΣ..
7. ΤΟ ΣΑΝΤΟΥΙΤΣ..
8. ΤΟ ΠΟΤΗΡΙ..

Στην ταβέρνα
At the restaurant

6

In this unit we will be focusing on the 'food' experience in Greece, looking at the language you'll need to order what you want, as well as highlighting some regional delicacies you might want to try.

Traveller's tip

Greeks enjoy eating out so it's no wonder there are so many different types of restaurants in Greece. Whether it is an informal meal in a taverna, a souvlaki in a souvlatzidiko (**σουβλατζίδικο**), mezedes and ouzo in a mezedopolio (**μεζεδοπωλείο**), ouzeri (**ουζερί**) or a fine meal in a top-class restaurant, Greeks take their time to enjoy it with friends or family.

A mezedopolio is a popular choice because you can order a variety of different dishes to taste with your ouzo or beer. Another good-value place to eat is a souvlatzidiko, in other words a place where you can eat or take away souvlaki. In a souvlatzidiko, though, there's not much variety in dishes – just the traditional souvlaki skewers or gyros wrapped in pitta, chips, Greek salad and tzatziki.

It is very easy to find lovely tavernas and restaurants for every budget and different regions have different specialities.

Something you'll need to be aware of is that Greeks eat late, usually between 9pm and 10pm, and sometimes even later.

The Mediterranean diet mainly consists of fresh fish, fresh vegetables and fruit and there is a huge variety of vegetarian dishes called ladera (**λαδερά**): gigandes, briami, domates gemistes, fasolakia kokkinista, aginares a la polita, araka, spanakorizo and dolmades are only some of the multitude of vegetarian dishes.

In this unit we will be focusing on expressions using **θα**, indicating something that takes place in the future. We will also look at the use of the accusative case (when something is having something done to it).

Listen up 1

Giorgos and Anna are at the taverna ordering a meal. Listen to the conversation they have with the waiter and see if you can pick out the different stages of the process. 34

Words and phrases 1

Τί θα πιείτε;	What will you drink?
το κρασί	the wine
κόκκινο	red
Διαλέξατε;	Have you chosen?
γιά την αρχή	to start
μία σαλάτα χωριάτικη	a Greek salad
ο γιγαντας / οι γίγαντες	butter beans in tomato sauce
η μελιτζανοσαλάτα	aubergine spread
το κυρίως πιάτο	main course
Τί θα φάτε;	What will you eat?
Θα πάρω ...	I will take ...
το κοκκινιστό κοτόπουλο	chicken in tomato sauce
το ρύζι	the rice
το μοσχάρι λεμονάτο	veal in lemon sauce
η πατάτα/οι πατάτες	potatoes
ο λογαριασμός	the bill

Unlocking the language 1

As you may have noticed the waiter is asking What will you drink?/**Τί θα πιείτε;**, What will you take?/**τί θα πάρετε;**, What will you eat?/**Τί θα φάτε;**. The little word **θα** indicates that the sentence is in the future. But this is not the only change; the form of the verb itself changes. For example, **θα φάω** is the verb **τρώω, θα πιώ** is the verb **πίνω**, and **θα πάρω** is the verb **παίρνω**.

Here are the three verbs conjugated in the present and the future tense:

τρώω to eat		πίνω to drink		παίρνω to take	
τρώω	θα φάω	πίνω	θα πιώ	παίρνω	θα πάρω
τρώς	θα φάς	πίνεις	θα πιείς	παίρνεις	θα πάρεις
τρώει	θα φάει	πίνει	θα πιεί	παίρνει	θα πάρει
τρώμε	θα φάμε	πίνουμε	θα πιούμε	παίρνουμε	θα πάρουμε
τρώτε	θα φάτε	πίνετε	θα πιείτε	παίρνετε	θα πάρετε
τρώνε	θα φάνε	πίνουν	θα πιούνε	παίρνουν	θα πάρουν

Your turn 1

Check your understanding. True or false? 34

		True	False
1.	Giorgos and Anna will drink red wine.	☐	☐
2.	For starters they will have only a Greek salad.	☐	☐
3.	For main course Giorgos has chosen mousaka.	☐	☐

Tip

The word 'portion' is **μερίδα**. When you order you can say 'a portion of chips' **μία μερίδα πατάτες τηγανητές** or you can just say **μία πατάτες τηγανητές**. The same is true if you want a portion of mousaka you can either say **μία μερίδα μουσακά** or **μία μουσακά**. As you will have noticed the indefinite article **μία** does not agree with the word 'chips' or 'mousaka' – it refers instead to the omitted word 'portion' **μερίδα**.

Find in the dialogue words and expressions to convey the following. Write your answers in the spaces provided: 34

1. Have you chosen? ....
2. main course ....
3. What have you got? ....
4. Is everything OK? ....
5. What will you drink? ....
6. aubergine salad ....
7. butter beans ....
8. I will take ... .

Pronunciation Tip

The letter combination '**αι**' sounds like the 'e' in ten and the letter combination '**ου**' sounds like the '**oo**' in soon. For example: **βεβαίως** (*veveos*) and **κοτόπουλο** (*kotopoolo*)

Say the following in Greek. Check your answers by listening to the audio track. 35

1. to start
2. What will you eat?
3. a portion
4. I will take ...
5. a bottle of red wine
6. the bill please

Listen carefully to the dialogue and answer the following questions: 36

1. What does the customer order to drink?
   a. A bottle of red wine and a beer
   b. A glass of water and a beer
   c. A glass of red wine and a bottle of water

2. What does the customer want to eat?
   a. Chicken with rice and a Greek salad
   b. Chicken with potatoes and a Greek salad
   c. Veal with potatoes and a Greek salad

Match the pictures with the dishes:

1. ντομάτες γεμιστές
2. μουσακά
3. ντολμάδες
4. μία σαλάτα χωριάτικη
5. σουβλάκι
6. πατάτες

a. 

b. 

c. 

d. 

e. 

f. 

Listen up 2

Listen to Nikos, Katia and Mary deciding what to eat in a restaurant. There's quite a bit of new vocabulary here so listen several times if you need to.

37

Words and phrases 2

ένα τραπέζι	table
το άτομο/άτομα	person/persons
κοντά	near
το παράθυρο	window
καθίστε	have a seat
το κορίτσι/τα κορίτσια	girl/girls
καλή ιδέα	good idea
προτιμώ	I prefer
το πρώτο πιάτο	first course
η σούπα λαχανικών	the vegetable soup
τα μανιτάρια με κρέμα	the mushrooms in cream
ο καπνιστός σολωμός	the smoked salmon
τα τηγανιτά καλαμαράκια	the fried calamari rings
το ψάρι	the fish
η γαρίδα/οι γαρίδες στο φούρνο	the prawn/the oven-cooked prawns
το κουτάλι	the spoon
καθαρό	clean
το μαχαιροπήρουνο (το μαχαίρι και το πηρούνι)	cutlery (knife and fork)
η πετσέτα	napkin
ακόμη	more/still

Unlocking the language 2

Did you notice that in the dialogue certain words were preceded by **τον** and **την** but in the Words and phrases 2 section above these same words appear differently? For example:

ο σολωμός/τον σολωμό
η κρέμα/την κρέμα
η σούπα /την σούπα

This is because these words are in two different cases: the nominative (**ονομαστική**) case and the accusative (**αιτιατική**) case. How do we know when to use one and when to use the other? The explanation is rather complicated but a simple way to think of it is that the nominative is when the noun is the subject of a sentence and the accusative is when the noun is the object of the sentence.

Salmon is a fish **Ο σολωμός είναι ψάρι** (nominative because 'salmon' is a subject)

Nicos will eat salmon **Ο Νίκος θα φάει τον σολωμό**. (accusative because "salmon" is the object)

The soup has vegetables **Η σούπα έχει λαχανικά** (nominative because (soup) is the subject.

I will take the soup **Θα πάρω την σούπα** (accusative because "soup" is the object.

What do you notice? In the first example the article is before the verb and in the second it is after the verb.

The neuter article **το** stays the same in both nominative and accusative cases.

Your turn 2

Check your understanding. Circle the correct answers: 37

1. The customers want a table for ...
   a. two people b. three people c. four people d. five people
2. The customers will drink ...
   a. red wine b. beer c. white wine d. ouzo
3. They need an extra ...
   a. glass b. knife c. fork d. napkin

Match the words with the corresponding pictures:

1. ο λογαριασμός
2. το ποτήρι
3. το κουτάλι
4. η πετσέτα
5. το πηρούνι
6. το μαχαίρι

a. 

b. 

c. 

d. 

e. 

f. 

How would you say the following in Greek?

38

1. a table for two, please
2. near the window
3. good idea
4. a bottle of white wine
5. I prefer red wine
6. I will take the soup

Listen carefully to the short dialogue and say whether the statements are true or false:

39

		True	False
1.	Nikos wants a spoon	☐	☐
2.	Mary asks for a clean knife	☐	☐
3.	Katia asks for another two glasses	☐	☐

Complete the dialogue below using words from the box: 40

άσπρο	παράθυρο	καθίστε	άτομα	μπουκάλι	τραπέζι

Nikos Ένα.................... γιά δύο.................... παρακαλώ

Waiter Βεβαίως

Nikos Έχετε ένα τραπέζί κοντά στο....................

Waiter Ορίστε,.................... τί θα πιείτε;

Nikos Ένα.................... .... κρασί.

Waiter Αμέσως.

Let's recap

Complete the sentences using the appropriate article:

1. ....Νίκος θα πάρει....................σολωμό. (ο, τον, η, την, το)
2. Θα φάω τα μανιτάρια με....................κρέμα. (ο, την, η, τον, το)
3. ....πετσέτα δεν είναι καθαρή. (ο, τον, το, η, την)
4. Εγώ προτιμώ....................σούπα. (η, το, την, ο, τον)
5. ....λογαριασμό παρακαλώ. (ο, τον, η, το, την)

Rearrange the following words into sentences:

1. τραπέζι στο ένα κοντά παράθυρο....................
2. σούπα ένα γιά κουτάλι την....................
3. πηρούνι δεν το καθαρό είναι....................
4. μπουκάλι θα ένα κόκκινο πάρουμε κρασί....................

ΣΠΑΡΟΙ
€4.00

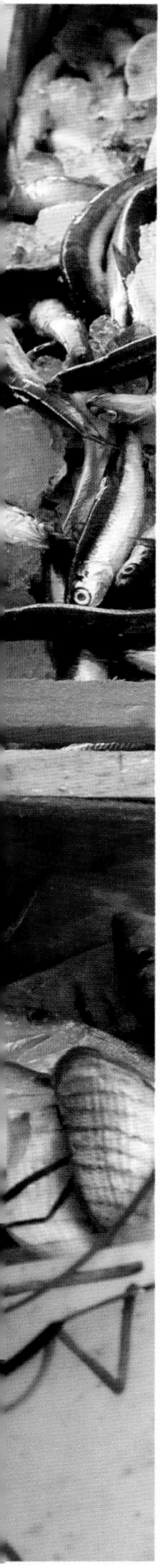

7 Ψωνίζοντας τρόφιμα Shopping for food

In this unit we will be focusing on the vocabulary you need when going shopping for food.

Traveller's tip

In Greece people prefer to do their shopping in small local shops rather than the big supermarkets. Every neighbourhood has its own bakery, greengrocer, dairy shop, chemist, butcher and fishmonger, as well as a small supermarket. Although prices tend to be higher in these small shops, the quality of the produce is usually much better. Most Greek neighbourhoods also have a weekly open market, where local food producers can sell their fresh fruit and vegetables direct to the public at much cheaper prices than the supermarkets. If you come across one of these local markets, do take the time for a leisurely stroll around – they are a feast for the eyes as well as the stomach.

In addition to these open-air markets, the big cities such as Athens, Thessaloniki and Patras have a permanent indoor market - often in a rather grand building taking up an entire city square. The indoor markets are bustling with stalls devoted to fresh Aegean fish, fruit and vegetables, or fresh meat; some even have bakeries and cafes in them.

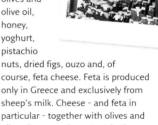

Many Greek products are well known worldwide: olives and olive oil, honey, yoghurt, pistachio nuts, dried figs, ouzo and, of course, feta cheese. Feta is produced only in Greece and exclusively from sheep's milk. Cheese - and feta in particular - together with olives and olive oil are very important in the Greek diet. Did you know Greeks are the biggest consumers of cheese in the world?

Opening times in the big supermarkets are from 9am to 9pm but many small shops close at 2:30pm or 3pm, re-opening in the afternoon from 5:30pm to 8:30pm three times a week on Tuesdays, Thursdays and Fridays. In Greece there is no Sunday trading, except in very 'touristy' places and even then only in the summer.

In this unit you will also learn how to talk about quantities and packaging and how to deal with adjectives.

Listen up 1

Nikos is at the grocer's buying a few groceries. Listen to the dialogue, then you'll find a series of explanations and exercises linked to it on the next few pages. 41

Words and phrases 1

το πακέτο	the packet
τα μακαρόνια	the pasta
το λάδι	the oil
το βούτυρο	the butter
η κονσέρβα/οι κονσέρβες.	the tin/tins
ένα τέταρτο	a quarter
η φέτα	the feta cheese
το γραμμάριο/τα γραμμάρια	the gram
η ελιά/οι ελιές	the olive/olives
η φέτα/οι φέτες	the slice/slices
το ζαμπόν	the ham
το βάζο	the jar
το μέλι	the honey

Unlocking the language 1

When speaking about packages and measures in Greek it is very simple: you just start with the packaging or weight and add the item. For example, a packet of rice is **ένα πακέτο ρύζι**, a bottle of milk is **ένα μπουκάλι γάλα**.

Your turn 1

Check your understanding: True or false? 41

		True	False
1.	Nikos wants a packet of spaghetti, a packet of butter, two tins of tomatoes and a bottle of oil.	☐	☐
2.	He also wants a quarter of olives.	☐	☐
3.	The bill is forty-two euros.	☐	☐

Match the items with the pictures:

1. ένα πακέτο βούτυρο
2. ένα μπουκάλι λάδι
3. ένα πακέτο ζάχαρη
4. ένα βάζο μέλι
5. δέκα φέτες ζαμπόν
6. ένα τέταρτο τυρί
7. ένα πακέτο μακαρόνια
8. μία κονσέρβα ντοματάκια

a. 

b. 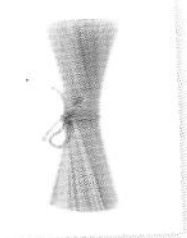

c. 

d. 

e. 

f. 

g. 

h. 

Pronunciation Tip

In Greek there are no single letters to convey 'b' and 'd'. To create the sound 'b' you must put the two letters 'μ' and 'π' together, as in the word 'grocer/**μπακάλης**' that you heard in Listen up 1. In the same way, for 'd' we put '**ν**' and '**τ**' together, as in the word '**ντοματάκια**'.

You are at the grocer's. Ask for the following items in Greek. You can check your answers by listening to the audio track: 42

1. a packet of sugar
2. a jar of coffee
3. Six slices of ham
4. a bottle of oil
5. 50 grams of olives
6. 100 grams of feta cheese

Listen to the short dialogue and tick the appropriate boxes: 43

	True	False
1. The customer wants a packet of butter and a packet of sugar.	☐	☐
2. The customer also wants 10 slices of ham and a jar of honey.	☐	☐
3. The items cost 30 euros.	☐	☐

Match the packaging on the left with the items on the right:

1. ένα πακέτο	a. τυρί
2. ένα μπουκάλι	b. ντοματάκια
3. ένα βαζο	c. ζαμπόν
4. μία κονσέρβα	d. ζάχαρη
5. 6 φέτες	e. λάδι
6. 250 γραμμάρια	f. μέλι

Listen up 2

Katia is buying some fruit at a market stall. Listen to the dialogue. 44

Words and phrases 2

ένα κιλό	a kilo
το μήλο/τα μήλα	the apple/the apples
το αχλάδι/τα αχλάδια	the pear/the pears
το ροδάκινο/τα ροδάκινα	the peach/the peaches
η φράουλα/οι φράουλες	the strawberry/the strawberries
το κεράσι/τα κεράσια	the cherry/the cherries
κάλά (plural neuter)	good
γλυκά (plural neuter)	sweets
½ κιλό	½ a kilo
το καρπούζι/τα καρπούζια	the watermelon/the watermelons
το πεπόνι	the melon
ένα τσαμπί σταφύλια	a bunch of grapes

Unlocking the language 2

Adjectives have to agree with the nouns they describe in number, gender and case. In English, this is easy because nouns have no gender but in Greek it's a little more complicated because there are three genders and four cases. For example, a small tomato is **μικρή ντομάτα**, but a small melon is **μικρό πεπόνι.**

In the dialogue that you've just listened to (Track 44), there are two adjectives in the plural neuter. This is because cherry, **κεράσι**, is neuter and here it is in the plural. Therefore the two adjectives used to describe cherries, **καλά** and **γλυκά**, are also in the plural.

Here are some adjectives you may find useful. The first version is the masculine, the second is the feminine and the third is the neuter:

small	μικρός/μικρή/μικρό
big	μεγάλος/μεγάλη/μεγάλο
medium	μέτριος/μέτρια/μέτριο
clean	καθαρός/καθαρή/καθαρό
dirty	βρώμικος/βρώμικη/βρώμικο
good	καλός/καλή/καλό
bad	κακός/κακή/κακό
easy	εύκολος/εύκολη/εύκολο
difficult	δύσκολος/δύσκολη/δύσκολο
sweet	γλυκός/γλυκιά/γλυκό
sour	ξινός/ξινή/ξινό
bitter	πικρός/πικρή/πικρό
pretty	όμορφος/όμορφη/όμορφο
clever	έξυπνος/έξυπνη/έξυπνο

Your turn 2

Check your understanding by filling in the missing words: 44

– Θα ήθελα ένα .... μήλα, ένα κιλό .... και μισό κιλό φράουλες

– Δυστυχώς δεν έχουμε φράουλες. Θέλετε τίποτε άλλο;

– Τα .... είναι καλά;

- Βεβαίως, είναι πολύ ....
- Τότε θα .... μισό κιλό κεράσια και ένα .... καρπούζι.
- Δεν έχουμε μέτρια καρπούζια, ... μεγάλα.
- Τότε θα πάρω ένα ...., μισό κιλό ροδάκινα και ένα .... σταφύλια.
- Ορίστε, θέλετε τίποτε άλλο;
- Όχι ευχαριστώ.
- Τριανταοκτώ .... όλα μαζί.
- Ορίστε .... ευρώ.
- Ορίστε δύο ευρώ ....

Match the items with the pictures:

1. ένα πεπόνι
2. ένα τσαμπί σταφύλια
3. ένα καρπούζι
4. ½ κιλό μήλα
5. 1 κιλό αχλάδια
6. 7 πορτοκάλια
7. ½ κιλο ροδάκινα
8. 1 κιλο κεράσια

a. 

b. 

c. 

d. 

e. 

f. 

g. 

h. 

You are at the greengrocer's. Ask for the following items in Greek. You can check your answers by listening to the audio track. 45

1. 10 oranges
2. ½ a kilo of cherries
3. 1 kilo of apples
4. a small watermelon
5. ½ a kilo of grapes
6. a sweet melon

Listen to the dialogue and say whether the following statements are true or false: 46

		True	False
1.	The customer wants a watermelon.	☐	☐
2.	He also wants a kilo of apples and half a kilo of pears.	☐	☐
3.	He bought six oranges.	☐	☐

Link the adjectives on the left with their opposites on the right:

1.	μικρός	a.	καθαρός
2.	καλός	b.	πικρός
3.	εύκολος	c.	μεγάλος
4.	γλυκός	d.	κακός
5.	βρώμικος	e.	δύσκολος

Let's recap

Re-arrange the order of the words to create complete sentences:

1. ήθελα βάζο θα μέλι πακέτο ένα βούτυρο ένα και ....

....

2. έχουμε κεράσια δεν δυστυχώς ....
3. πεπόνια ένα και καρπούζι δύο ....
4. πολύ πορτοκάλια είναι τα γλυκά ....

Choose the correct form of each adjective to complete the sentences:

1. Τα αχλάδια είναι ....

   a. μικρό b. μικρή c. μικρός d. μικρά

2. Το πεπόνι είναι ....

   a. μικρό b. μικρός c. μικρά d. μικρή

3. Ο Γιώργος είναι ....

   a. έξυπνη b. έξυπνα c. έξυπνος d. έξυπνο

4. Η Κατερίνα είναι ....

   a. όμορφος b. όμορφη c. όμορφα d. όμορφο

Fill in the gaps with the correct form of adjective. (Some adjectives may be in the plural.)

1. Θα ήθελα ένα .... βάζο καφέ. (μικρός)
2. Δώστε μου δυό .... μπουκάλια νερό (μεγάλος).
3. Αυτά τα πορτοκάλια είναι .... (ξινός)
4. Μου δίνετε μία .... (καθαρός) πετσέτα;
5. Η μηλόπιττα είναι ....(γλυκός).
6. Η Μαρία είναι .... (έξυπνος) και .... (όμορφος)
7. Θα ήθελα πέντε .... (μέτριος) αχλάδια.
8. Η .... (μικρός) μπύρα κάνει 1 ευρώ, η .... (μεγάλος) κάνει 1.50 ευρώ.

Πάμε γιά ψώνια; Shopping for clothes

8

In this unit we will be focusing on vocabulary that relates to clothes – garments, sizes, colours, etc.

Traveller's tip

The first thing you'll notice in big Greek cities is that whilst some large chains are present, they are less prevalent than would be the case in other European countries. Whereas the UK, for example, is infamous for having branches of the same shops on every high street, Greece's shopping streets are full of traditional, family-run shops and small businesses.

Opening hours for small shops are Monday, Wednesday and Saturday, 9am to 3pm, and Tuesday, Thursday and Friday, 9am to 2pm and re-opening from 5:30pm to 8:30pm. Shopping centres open longer hours and do not close for lunch.

Shoes, handbags and leather goods in general are very stylish, very good quality and good value for money in Greece, and if you are fond of designer clothes or big brand names you should head for Kolonaki, Kifissia or Glyfada in Athens. Parts of downtown Athens is now barred to cars and pedestrians can walk in safety. The main street for clothes shopping - Ermou Street - has become like a street fair, or high-class bazaar, with thousands of people, street musicians and stalls selling hot chestnuts in winter and corn cobs in summer.

Whether you're a shopaholic or a retail novice, a dip into the sights, sounds and smells of Greek shopping is always a colourful experience.

In this unit you will learn the Greek words for some colours and also how to use the comparative and superlative cases – in other words, how to say that you want something bigger or smaller.

Listen up 1

A customer in a boutique wants to buy a new skirt. Listen to the dialogue to see how she gets on. Try to pick out the price of the items she buys.

47

Words and phrases 1

η φούστα	the skirt
το μέγεθος	the size
προβάρω	to try
το νούμερο	the size/number
η έκπτωση	sales/the discount
η μπλούζα	the blouse
τα μετρητά	the cash
η κάρτα	the card
το φόρεμα	the dress
μεταξωτό	in silk

Unlocking the language 1

Colours are adjectives and therefore they have to agree with the item they are describing so if you want a red skirt you should say **μια κόκκινη φούστα** but if you want a red shirt you should say **ένα κόκκινο πουκάμισο.** If you want to make things easier you can say that you want a garment in a specific colour, for example: I would like a skirt in red/**Θα ήθελα μια φούστα σε κόκκινο.**

The word 'colour' is neuter so when you are referring to colours you must use the neuter.

white **άσπρο**

black **μαύρο**

green **πράσινο**

yellow **κίτρινο**

red **κόκκινο**

blue **μπλέ**

orange **πορτοκαλί**

pink **ρόζ**

brown **καφέ**

grey **γκρί**

purple **μώβ**

The following colours are invariable: **μπλέ, πορτοκαλί, ροζ, καφέ, γκρί, μωβ**

Your turn 1

Check your understanding. True or false? 47

		True	False
1.	The customer wants a skirt in size 38 or 40.	☐	☐
2.	The changing room is on the left.	☐	☐
3.	The skirt has a 20% discount.	☐	☐

Find expressions in the dialogue to convey the following: 47

1. What size do you wear?
2. The changing rooms are here on the right.
3. I prefer the red.
4. It has a 20% discount
5. How are you going to pay?
6. cash

Pronunciation Tip

The letter 'g' in Greek is composed of two letters. For a soft 'g' as in 'gel', you put '**τ**' and '**ζ**' together. For a hard 'g' as in 'garage' you put '**γ**' and '**κ**' together, or you put two '**γ**' together. Example: **γκρί** You can never start a word with a double '**γ**'. Example: **αγγούρι**

How would you say the following colours in Greek? Check your answers by listening to the audio track. 48

1. red
2. blue
3. green
4. brown
5. yellow
6. white
7. pink
8. black

Listen to the short dialogue and say whether the following statements are true or false: 49

		True	False
1.	The customer wants a yellow skirt.	☐	☐
2.	She also wants a black blouse.	☐	☐
3.	She wears size 36.	☐	☐

Link the colours in English with the colours in Greek:

1. black	a. γκρί
2. purple	b. πράσινο
3. pink	c. μαύρο
4. yellow	d. μώβ
5. green	e. ρόζ
6. orange	f. άσπρο
7. grey	g. πορτοκαλί
8. white	h. κίτρινο

Listen up 2

Another shopping trip. This time the customer is looking at men's clothes. Listen to the dialogue and then do the exercise below to check how much you've understood. 50

Refer to the Words and phrases 2 section for help with any unfamiliar words.

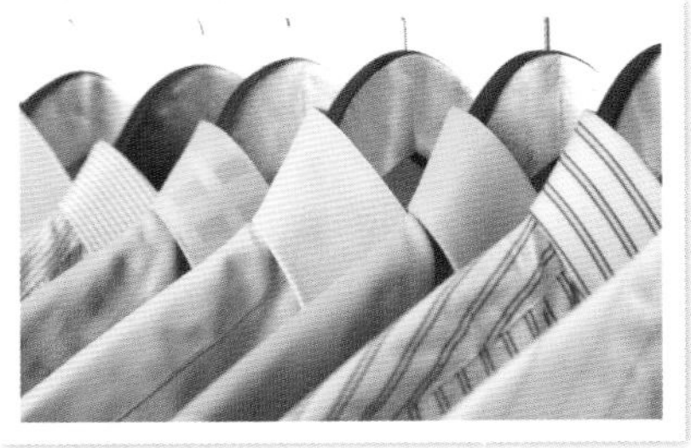

Words and phrases 2

το παντελόνι	the trousers
είναι πολύ ακριβό	it is very expensive
μικρό	small
πιό φτηνό	cheaper
το πουκάμισο	the shirt
βαμβακερό	in cotton
η ζώνη	the belt
δερμάτινη	in leather
η πιό φτηνή	the cheapest

Unlocking the language 2

When you want to express a comparison you just add the word **πιό** in front of the adjective, like this: **πιό μικρό**, **πιό φτηνό**. If you want to say that something is the cheapest, the smallest, etc., you just add the article of the noun in front of **πιό**, as in these examples: **η πιό φτηνή ζώνη**, **το πιό φτηνό πουκάμισο:**

Your turn 2

Check your understanding. True or false? 50

		True	False
1.	The customer wants a pair of trousers in blue or grey.	☐	☐
2.	The blue trousers are a bit too big.	☐	☐
3.	The customer wants a leather belt too.	☐	☐

Find expressions in the dialogue to convey the following: 50

1. It's a little bit small.
2. Have you got a cheaper one?
3. I would like a white cotton shirt.
4. We only have it in grey.
5. Do you like this belt?
6. It's the cheapest we have.

How would you say the following in Greek?: 51

1. I would like a blue pair of trousers.
2. The yellow dress is a little too small.
3. leather belt
4. Have you got a cheaper shirt?

Listen to the dialogue and tick the appropriate boxes: 52

		True	False
1.	The customer wants a black pair of trousers.	☐	☐
2.	They have his size in brown and grey but not in black.	☐	☐
3.	He also wants a black leather belt.	☐	☐
4.	There is a 10% discount.	☐	☐

Link these garments with the correct picture:

1. ζώνη
2. φόρεμα
3. φούστα
4. μπλούζα
5. παντελόνι
6. πουκάμισ

a. 

b. 

c. 

d. 

e. 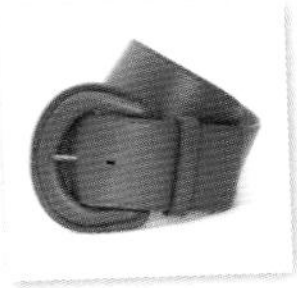

f. 

Let's recap

Match the adjectives on the right with the nouns on the left:

1. ένα κόκκινο	a. φούστες
2. μία μεταξωτή	b. πουκάμισα
3. μία δερμάτινη	c. μπλούζα
4. δύο βαμβακερά	d. φόρεμα
5. δύο βαμβακερές	e. ζώνη

Re-arrange the words to construct correct sentences:

1. μικρή θα φούστα πιό μία ήθελα ....
2. το είναι ακριβό παντελόνι λίγο αυτό ....
3. είναι έχουμε αυτή πιό η μπλούζα που φτηνή ....
4. 10% αυτό έχει το έκπτωση φόρεμα ....

Και λίγη κουλτούρα
A bit of culture

9

In this unit we'll take a trip to a Greek museum, looking at what's on offer, what you can expect to pay, and how to say what you need to say there. We will also have a look at buying tickets for the theatre.

Traveller's tip

Anywhere you go in Greece, one thing is certain: there are museums, archaeological sites and ancient ruins to visit in every city or town. Opening hours vary depending on the time of year, opening earlier and closing later in the summer months. Entry to museums varies too. Some museums do not charge an entry fee, while others charge up to 7 euros, and some museums are closed on Mondays.

While visiting Athens the New Acropolis Museum is worth seeing. It is located just 2km from Syntagma Square in the historical area of Makriyannis. The Museum is open Tuesday to Sunday, 8am to 8pm, and the admission fee is 1 euro. It opened in June 2009 and has approximately 4,000 artifacts on display. For the first time ever, all the surviving treasures of the Acropolis can be seen together in one place. Other museums that are worth a visit include the National Archaeological Museum, the Benaki Museum, the Museum of Cycladic Art, the Byzantine Museum, and many more.

If you want to immerse yourself in Greek culture then the Athens and Edidaurus Festival can offer a huge variety of events, from pop concerts to classical music, ballet and ancient Greek comedies and tragedies.

In Greece there are still a few open-air cinemas. We call them **θερινό σινεμά** and they show two performances each evening, one from 9pm to 11pm and then a late-night one from 11pm to 1am. Open-air cinemas are an ideal way to spend a hot summer's evening, especially as foreign films are in the original version with Greek subtitles. You can drink a beer or soft drink, or eat souvlaki or crisps while watching a good film.

In this unit you will learn how to express likes and dislikes, and also how to express your intentions and plans using the subjunctive form.

Listen up 1

Peter wants to go to the new Acropolis Museum and asks the hotel receptionist for directions. Listen to the dialogue. 53

Words and phrases 1

μπορώ να σας δώσω	I can give you
ο χάρτης	the map
εκτός	except
μέσω Ίντερνετ	via internet
αν σας αρέσουν	if you like (many)
αρχαίος/αρχαίοι	ancient
ο συγγραφέας/οι συγγραφείς	the writer
η παράσταση	the performance
αν έχετε χρόνο	if you have time
τα κεντρικά ταμεία	the box office

Unlocking the language 1

Likes and dislikes

When you want to say that you like or dislike something, you use the expression **μου αρέσει** or **μου αρέσουν**. You use **μου αρέσει** when you are referring to one person or item and **μου αρέσουν** if you are referring to more than one. For example:

I like pop music/**μου αρέσει η ποπ μουσική**, I like pop concerts/**μου αρέσουν οι συναυλίες πόπ**.

Μου αρέσει πάρα πολύ	I like it very much
Μου αρέσει πολύ	I like it a lot
Μου αρέσει αρκετά	I quite like it
Μου αρέσει λίγο	I don't mind it
Δεν μου αρέσει	I don't like it
Δεν μου αρέσει πολύ	I don't like it very much
Δεν μου αρέσει καθόλου	I don't like it at all

If you want to say 'you like ...', you say **σου αρέσει**, for 'he likes ...' you say **του αρέσει**, for 'she likes ...' it's **της αρέσει**. 'We like' is **μας αρέσει**, 'you like' (plural or formal) is **σας αρέσει** and 'they like' is **τους αρέσει**.

Your turn 1

Check your understanding. True or false? 53

		True	False
1.	The Acropolis Museum is open on Mondays.	☐	☐
2.	You can buy e-tickets to visit the Acropolis Museum.	☐	☐
3.	Peter likes ancient Greek writers.	☐	☐

Find expressions in the dialogue that convey the following: 53

1. I can give you this map.
2. It is open every day except Mondays.
3. From eight in the morning until eight in the evening.
4. You can buy tickets at the museum's box office.
5. I suggest you go to the Herod Atticus Theatre.
6. I like ancient Greek writers very much.
7. It is a very good performance.
8. If you have time, you can go to Epidaurus.

Pronunciation Tip

The expressions **μου αρέσει, σου αρέσει** and **του αρέσει** can also be said as **μ'αρέσει, σ'αρέσει** and **τ'αρέσει**.

How would you say the following in Greek? Check your answers by listening to the audio track. 54

1. I like classical music a lot.
2. I quite like jazz.
3. I don't mind pop music.
4. I don't like rap music at all.
5. I like Jane Austen and Charles Dickens very much.
6. I don't like beach parties.

Listen to the dialogue and select the correct answer: 55

1. Maria likes
   a. Elton John
   b. Michael Jackson
2. Giorgos prefers
   a. Classical music
   b. Jazz
3. Giorgos doesn't like
   a. Louis Armstrong
   b. Elton John

Match the pictures with the names of the famous places:

1. Παρθενών
2. Θέατρο της Επιδαύρου

3. Λυκαβητός
4. Θέατρο Ηρώδου του Αττικού
5. Παναθηναϊκό στάδιο
6. Στήλες του Ολυμπίου Διός
7. Βουλή των Ελλήνων

a.

b.

c.

d.

e.

f.

g.

Listen up 2

Peter decides to go to the Herod Atticus Theatre in Athens to watch the ancient Greek comedy 'Birds' with his family. Now he is at the box office buying tickets. 56

Words and phrases 2

οι Όρνιθες	a play by Aristophanes called 'Birds'
κανονικό/κανονικά	regular
παιδικό	child's
αύριο	tomorrow
η σειρά	row
το κέντρο	centre
το πρόγραμμα	the programme
η κωμωδία	the comedy
ο Αριστοφάνης	Aristophanes: Ancient Greek writer

Unlocking the language 2

As you may have noticed some verbs are preceded by **να**. This corresponds to the English word 'to': I want to go home/**Θέλω να πάω σπίτι**. This little word **να** is used with verbs expressing a wish, a must, a need – for example: You can go/**Μπορείτε να πάτε**. In Greek, this is called using the 'subjunctive'. The subjunctive is formed in the same way as the future tense; the only difference is that instead of **θα**, you use **να**.

Future:	I will go	**Θα πάω**
Subjunctive:	I want to go	**Θέλω να πάω**

Your turn 2

Select the correct answer to check your understanding: 56

1. Peter wants three tickets for:
   a. tonight
   b. tomorrow night
2. The seats are:
   a. in the centre, row five
   b. in the centre, row fifteen
3. The play starts:
   a. at nine
   b. around nine

Find expressions in the dialogue that convey the following: 56

1. for tomorrow evening
2. Would you like me to give you a programme?
3. I would like to buy this book too.
4. the performance

Say the following in Greek: 57

1. Say you would like two tickets for 'Lysistrata' for tomorrow evening.
2. Ask what time does the performance start?
3. Ask how much does the programme cost?

Listen carefully and answer the questions that follow: 58

1. Which play does the tourist want to see? ....
2. Which day does he want to go? ....
3. At what time does the play start? ....

Match the words with the pictures:

1. το θέατρο
2. η τραγωδία
3. το πρόγραμμα
4. η κωμωδία
5. το θερινό σινεμά
6. το εισιτήριο

a. 

b. 

c. 

d. 

e. 

f. 

Let's recap

Put the words in the following sentences into the correct order:

1. ανοιχτό Ακρόπολης το είναι μουσείο δεν Δευτέρα την της ....
....
2. αγοράσω μουσείο να εισιτήρια θέλω δύο Μπενάκη το γιά ....
....
3. Αριστοφάνη οι είναι κωμωδία του ''Όρνιθες' ....
....
4. σινεμά αρέσει το πολύ μου θερινό ....
....

Match the word on the left with the appropriate words on the right:

1.	το μουσείο της Ακρόπολης	a.	προτιμώ την ποπ
2.	Μου αρέσει πολύ	b.	στο θέατρο της Επιδαύρου
3.	Η Λυσιστράτη είναι	c.	είναι κλειστό την Δευτέρα
4.	Η παράσταση της «Ηλέκτρας» είναι	d.	το θερινό σινεμά
5.	Δεν μου αρέσει η τζαζ	e.	κωμωδία του Αριστοφάνη

Select from the list below the appropriate expression to complete the dialogue:

a. Καλησπέρα,
b. Και τί ώρα τελειώνει;
c. Πόσο κάνει;
d. Τί ώρα τελειώνουμε;
e. Καλημέρα,
f. Ευχαριστώ πολύ,
g. Παρακαλώ,
h. Γιά πότε;
i. Πόσο κάνουν;
j. Τί ώρα αρχίζει η παράσταση;

1. ....

- Καλημέρα. Θα ήθελα δύο εισιτήρια γιά την «Μήδεια» παρακαλώ.

2. ....

- Γιά αύριο το βράδυ.
- Βεβαίως, ορίστε

3. ....

- 30 ευρώ

4. ....

- Στίς 8:00 το βράδυ

5. ....

- Στις 10:30

6. ....

- Παρακαλώ. Καλή διασκέδαση!

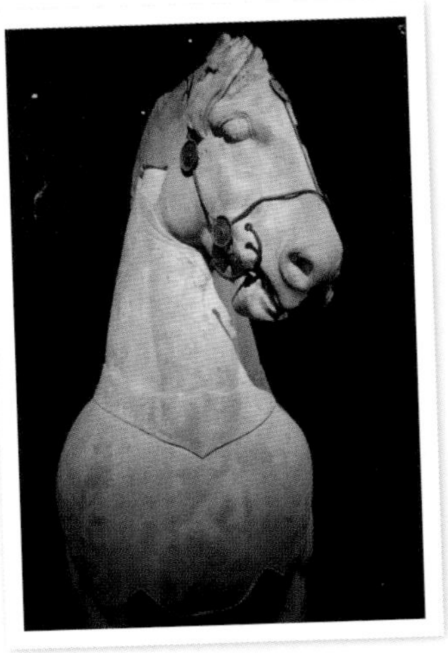

Νυχτερινή ζωή
Nightlife

10

In this unit we will focus on Greek nightlife and going to a club or bar after dinner.

Traveller's tip

We've all heard stories of revellers coming back from Rhodes, Cos or Corfu and gushing about how late they were able to stay out drinking. In fact, away from the tourist areas, the purpose of Greece's relatively relaxed licensing laws is to allow people to unwind gently, unhurriedly, having enjoyed a good meal beforehand. Eating and drinking generally go hand in hand in Greece, which makes going out for the evening a very enjoyable experience.

Greece has many different types of bars. There are the normal bars that play soft music and serve the usual variety of alcoholic and non-alcoholic drinks and cocktails, as well as coffee, and which sometimes have live music – jazz, latin, rock, or traditional Greek music. In cities these bars will generally start to shut down around midnight. After this, many Greeks will head for what is known as 'the after', a term borrowed from English. 'Afters' stay open until 1am or later – sometimes as late as 3am or 4am – and they play music very loud. In Greece we also have 'bouzoukia' (**μπουζούκια**). They open at about midnight and play live Greek music.

It's worth noting that Greece's public smoking policy requires pubs and bars smaller than 70 square metres to declare themselves either smoking or non-smoking, and stick to it. The larger clubs and bars are non-smoking, but some have designated areas devoted to each preference.

Of course, some of the tourist nightlife areas can be a bit rowdy, but away from those areas a normal night out in Greece, however late you finish, is likely to be an enjoyable, peaceful affair.

In this unit you will learn how to use the expression 'any' and how to talk about small or little things.

Listen up 1

Giorgos and Kostas are deciding where to go tonight. Listen to the dialogue and see if you can pick out where they head for. You can refer to Words and phrases 1 to help you. 59

Words and phrases 1

σήμερα	today
τίποτα	nothing
το μπαρ	the bar
το μπαράκι	the little bar
το ποτό	the drink
η πλατεία	the square
παίζει (παίζω)	to play
το συγκρότημα	the group
λοιπόν	so
το συγκροτηματάκι	the little group
καταπληκτικό	extraordinary
υπέροχο	superb
ο νεαρός	the young man
η τραγουδίστρια	the singer (female)
φανταστική	fantastic
η φωνή	the voice
ο πάγος	the ice

Unlocking the language 1

-**άκι** is a suffix added to a noun to mean 'little', for example: **το παιδί/το παιδάκι**, child/little child. Whatever the gender of the noun, when -**άκι** is added the gender changes into neuter: **ο σκύλος/το σκυλάκι**, the dog/the little dog.

Your turn 1

Check your understanding. True or false? 59

		True	False
1.	There are only two bars nearby.	☐	☐
2.	They will meet at about 11pm to go to a Latin bar.	☐	☐
3.	Kostas will drink a whisky with ice.	☐	☐

Find expressions in the dialogue that convey the following: 59

1. Shall we go for a drink?
2. Why not?
3. So, see you tonight at around 11pm.
4. How do you like it?
5. This little group is superb.
6. The singer has a fantastic voice.

Pronunciation Tip

Double consonants do not change the pronunciation of words except for double '**γ**', which becomes 'g' as in the word 'Greece'.

How would you say the following expressions in Greek? Check your answers by listening to the audio track. 60

1. What will you drink?
2. I will take a whisky with a lot of ice.
3. See you tonight around 10pm.
4. This little group is very good.

Listen to the dialogue and say whether the following statements are true or false: 61

		True	False
1.	There are a lot of good bars in the square.	☐	☐
2.	'Lotos' has Greek music.	☐	☐
3.	They will meet at 10pm.	☐	☐

Put the words in the following sentences in the correct order:

1. βράδυ κάνεις τί σήμερα το ....
2. μπαράκι κανένα καλό ξέρεις ....
3. πολλά γύρω έχει εδώ μπαράκια ....
4. παίζει ο σαξόφωνο που καλός νεαρός πολύ είναι ....

....

Listen up 2

A group of friends are deciding whether to go to a club to dance. Listen carefully, as they'll be buying a round of drinks – a handy thing to know how to do! 62

Words and phrases 2

Τί λέτε;	What are you saying?
χορέψω (χορεύω)	to dance
αποκλείεται	out of the question
κουρασμένος	tired
ξενυχτήσω (ξενυχτάω)	have a late night
μόνο	only
βαρελίσια μπύρα	draught beer

Unlocking the language 2

The expression 'any' in Greek is **κανένας**, but it depends on the noun you are referring to. If you are referring to a masculine word, it is **κανένας**, if you are referring to a feminine word it is **καμμία**, and if you are referring to a neuter word it is **κανένα**. So, if you want to say: 'Do you have any beer?', it will be **Έχετε καμμία μπύρα**; and if you want to say 'Have you got any whisky?', you will say **Έχετε κανένα ουίσκυ**.

Your turn 2

Check your understanding of the dialogue. True or false? 62

		True	False
1.	The two ladies like music.	☐	☐
2.	Kostas wants to go to bouzoukia.	☐	☐
3.	The two men order beer.	☐	☐

Find expressions in the dialogue that convey the following: 62

1. Shall we go to a disco?
2. We can go to both.
3. I'm very tired.
4. Shall we get going?
5. It's late and we all work tomorrow.

How would you say the following in Greek?

1. I'll take a glass of draught beer.
2. I'm very tired.
3. Out of the question.
4. Shall we go? It's late.

Listen to the dialogue and tick the correct boxes: (CD 63)

		True	False
1.	The four friends will go dancing in 'Dreams'.	☐	☐
2.	The 'Dreams' disco is too far.	☐	☐
3.	The music in 'Gazi' is very good.	☐	☐
4.	The disc jockey in 'Gazi' is from Venezuela.	☐	☐

Match the pictures with the appropriate drink:

1. ένα ουίσκυ με πάγο
2. ένα ποτήρι σαμπάνια
3. ένα μπουκάλι μπύρα
4. ένα κοκτέιλ
5. ένα ποτήρι μπύρα

a.

b.

c.

d.

e.

Let's recap

Change the following words and make them 'little'. Remember you need to add -άκι at the end and change the gender to neuter. Example: the cat/the little cat, η γάτα/το γατάκι.

1. το χέρι ....
2. το παιδί ....
3. ο αδελφός/η αδελφή ....
4. το σπίτι ....
5. το ούζο ....
6. το κρασί ....

Fill in the gaps with the appropriate form of 'any':

1. η πορτοκαλάδα θέλεις .... πορτοκαλάδα;
2. το νερό θα πάρω .... νερό.
3. η τυρόπιττα τρώμε .... τυρόπιττα;
4. το μπαρ πάμε σε .... μπαρ;
5. η μπύρα θέλεις .... μπύρα;
6. το κρασί πίνουμε .... κρασί;

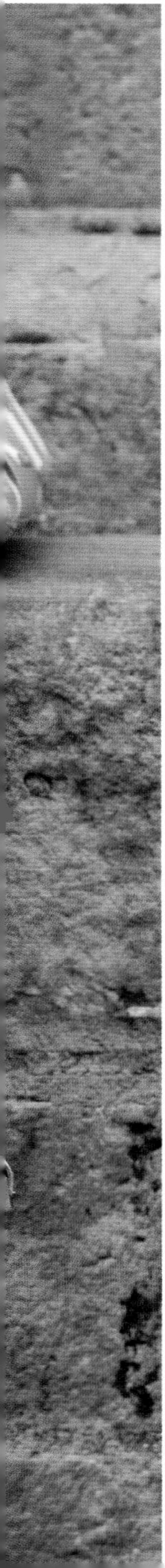

11

Να μην χαθούμε ... Keeping in touch

In this unit we will revise numbers up to 100 and learn numbers from 100 to 1000. We will also look at the language of communication – phones, mobiles, texting and emails.

Traveller's tip

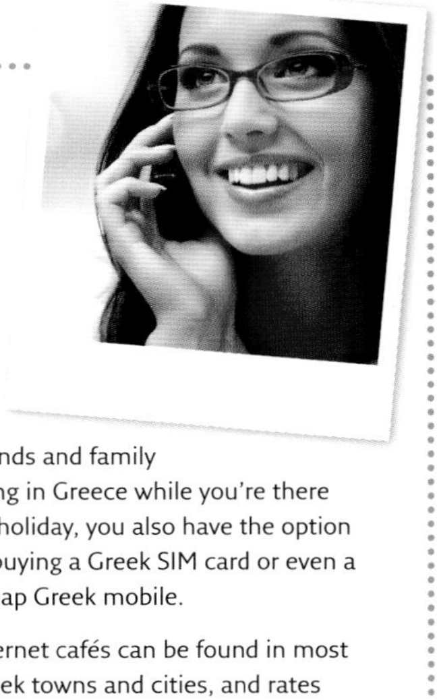

It's great to make friends in Greece during your visit, and to keep in touch once you're back in your own country. It's an ideal way to practise the language, as well as giving you a social platform for future visits.

These days, your mobile phone – **το κινητό** – and email – **ημέηλ** – are the two most common tools for keeping in touch. In fact, you may already have used email in Greece – in an internet café – and may be used to phoning or texting home by mobile.

You'll see that Greeks are every bit as technologically savvy as foreign visitors are, and that there are a range of telephony companies working in tandem with your mobile service provider back home. Don't be surprised if, when you switch on your mobile on emerging from the airport in Greece, your screen lights up with the name of a local telephone network.

Roaming rates have dropped spectacularly over the last couple of years, but if you want to contact friends and family living in Greece while you're there on holiday, you also have the option of buying a Greek SIM card or even a cheap Greek mobile.

Internet cafés can be found in most Greek towns and cities, and rates tend to be very reasonable. You may even find your hotel has internet facilities available to guests.

When you are in Greece and you want to make a phone call, you must always dial the area code first, even if you are ringing from the same area.

In this unit you will practise telephone numbers and you will also learn a little about the use of the future tense.

Listen up 1

Giorgos, Paul and Alice are swapping phone numbers at the end of their holiday. Listen out for the patterns of how phone numbers are expressed, but don't worry if it feels unfamiliar at first - the exercises on the next few pages will help you practise them. 64

Words and phrases 1

γράψω (γράφω)	to write
πρέπει	must
όμως	but
ο κωδικός	the code
τοπικός	area
πεντακόσια	five hundred
τελευταίο	last
το ποτηράκι	the small glass
η ποικιλία	a dish with a variety of meze
η πτήση	the flight
ο χρόνος	length of time, year

Unlocking the language 1

Numbers

Here are the Greek numbers up to 1000.

100	εκατό	600	εξακόσια
200	διακόσια	700	επτακόσια
300	τριακόσια	800	οκτακόσια
400	τετρακόσια	900	εννιακόσια
500	πεντακόσια	1000	χίλια

Telephone numbers in Greece are said in many ways, sometimes in units, other times in tens or in hundreds. For example: 210, which is the area code for Athens, can be said either as two hundred and ten (210) or as two, ten (2 10). Greek telephone numbers are 10 digits including the area code. In Athens the area code is 210 so the telephone number will be seven digits, eg. 210 32 45 123. In other areas where the area code is five digits long, the telephone number of the person or business is also five digits, eg. 22460 33 123. Greek mobile numbers start with six and the most common networks start with 697, 694 or 693.

Tips

Ευχαριστώ means 'thank you' and is stressed at the end.
Have you noticed the word **Ευχαρίστως**? It means 'with pleasure'.
It is stressed on the **ι** rather than the **ω** and has an **ς** at the end.

The word **χρόνος** means 'year' or 'length of time'.
So if you want to say 'in one year' you will say: **σε ένα χρόνο**
If you want to say you are short of time you will say **δεν έχω χρόνο.**

In the same way the word **ώρα** means 'hour' or 'time'. So if you want to ask 'what time is it?' you will say: **τί ώρα είναι;** But if you want to say you haven't got time, you can say: **δεν έχω ώρα**

In your dialogue **έχουμε ώρα** and **έχουμε χρόνο** both mean 'we have time'.

Your turn 1

Check your understanding by selecting the appropriate options: 64

		True	False
1.	Alice doesn't have a mobile phone.	☐	☐
2.	Alice's and Paul's flight is at 4pm.	☐	☐
3.	They will go to the airport by bus because		
	a. It's cheaper.	☐	☐
	b. They have plenty of time.	☐	☐

Find expressions in the dialogue that convey the following: 64

1. Will you give me your telephone number?
2. But you must dial the code for the UK.
3. What time is your flight?
4. We have plenty of time.

Pronunciation Tip

Some long nouns stressed on the third syllable from the end, take an extra stress at the end when followed by the possessive pronouns. For example: your telephone/**το τηλέφωνό σου**.

How would you say the following telephone numbers in Greek? You can listen to the audio track to check if you are right. 65

1. My telephone number is 22 450 16 139.
2. My mobile is 6 97 98 36 229.

Listen and write down the telephone numbers you hear: 66

1. ....
2. ....
3. ....

Match the numbers on the left to the corresponding digits on the right:

1.	διακόσια εβδομήντα τρία	a.	839
2.	εξακόσια σαράντα ένα	b.	1515
3.	πεντακόσια είκοσι οκτώ	c.	273
4.	τριακόσια εξήντα δύο	d.	641
5.	οκτακόσια τριάντα εννέα	e.	362
6.	χίλια πεντακόσια δέκα πέντε	f.	528

Listen up 2

67

This time, the three friends are saying their final goodbyes at the airport. Listen to the dialogue and refer to Words and phrases 2 for help with any words you can't pick out first time.

Words and phrases 2

το μήνυμα	the message
θα στείλω (στέλνω)	will send
από το δικό του	from his
μόλις	as soon as/just
γιά όλα	for everything
δεν κάνει τίποτε	don't mention it
πάλι	again
του χρόνου	next year
θα έρθω (έρχομαι)	I will come
θα περιμένω (περιμένω)	I will be waiting/expecting
θα προσπαθήσω (προσπαθώ)	I will try
Καλό ταξίδι	Have a safe journey.
Καλή αντάμωση	Till we meet again.

Unlocking the language 2

It is very easy to recognise the future tense because there is always the little word **θα** in front of the verb. Most of the common verbs are irregular and therefore it is simpler to give a list of these verbs in the future tense rather than explain in detail how to form them.

Verb	Present tense	Future tense
To be	**είμαι**	**θα είμαι**
To have	**έχω**	**θα έχω**
To eat	**τρώω**	**θα φάω**
To drink	**πίνω**	**θα πιώ**
To take	**παίρνω**	**θα πάρω**
To give	**δίνω**	**θα δώσω**
To bring	**φέρνω**	**θα φέρω**

Your turn 2

Check your understanding. True or false? 67

		True	False
1.	Alice will send Giorgos an SMS from London.	☐	☐
2.	Alice will email Giorgos with the pictures.	☐	☐
3.	Giorgos will go to London next year.	☐	☐

Find expressions in the dialogue to convey the following: 67

1. I don't have a mobile.
2. I will send you the pictures tomorrow.
3. Thank you for everything.
4. Safe journey.
5. Will you come again next year?
6. Till we meet again.

Say the following expressions in Greek, then listen to track 68 to check your answers. 68

1. I will text you from London.
2. Have you got my email?
3. We'll come again next year.

Listen to the dialogue and answer the questions that follow: 69

1. At what time is his flight?
   a. 4pm
   b. 6pm
   c. 6am
2. What is his destination?
   a. Athens
   b. London
   c. Argos
3. His mobile number is:
   a. 6 94 33 45 895
   b. 6 94 32 44 895
   c. 6 94 33 44 895

Let's recap

Select the appropriate verb from the list to complete the sentences:

θα φάτε   θα πιούν   θα πάω   θα πάρουμε   θα έρθει   θα δώσεις

1. Ο Γιώργος και η Άννα.................... μπύρα.
2. Πότε.................... ο Πώλ από την Αγγλία;
3. .... στην Έλλη αυτό το βιβλίο.
4. .... στο σινεμά με την Μαίρη.
5. Τί.................... σήμερα το βράδυ;
6. .... τρείς μπύρες.

Write the following numbers in words:

1. 329 ....
2. 482 ....
3. 164 ....
4. 746 ....
5. 288 ....
6. 651 ....

Select the appropriate form of the verbs in the future tense:

1. Ο Γιώργος .... τηλέφωνο στις 8:00.
   a. θα πάρω b. θα πάρει c. θα πάρετε d. θα πάρουμε
2. Η Αννα και η Μαρία .... στο σινεμά το βράδυ.
   a. θα πάνε b. θα πάω c. θα πας d. θα πάμε
3. Κυρία Μακρή, ... έναν καφέ;
   a. θα πιεί b. θα πιείς c. θα πιείτε d. θα πιούν
4. Γιώργο, ... μία τυρόπιτα;
   a. θα φάω b. θα φάει c. θα φας d. θα φάμε
5. Ο Νταλάρας .... μία συναυλία στο Ηρώδειο.
   a. θα δώσουν b. θα δώσεις c. θα δώσετε d. θα δώσει

Put the words in the correct order:

1. πολύ όλα ευχαριστούμε γιά ....
2. κάνει δεν τίποτα ....
3. ώρα τί πτήση είναι η σας; ....
4. στείλω Λονδίνο μόλις θα μήνυμα στο σου ένα φτάσω ....

Correct the mistakes in the following numbers:

1.	εξακόσια πενήντα τέσσερα	644	should be ....
2.	χίλια διακόσια ενενήντα οκτώ	1278	should be ....
3.	εννιακόσια είκοσι επτά	921	should be ....
4.	τετρακόσια ογδόντα ένα	489	should be ....
5.	πεντακόσια εξήντα δύο	532	should be ....
6.	εκατόν δώδεκα	110	should be ....
7.	διακόσια εβδομήντα έξι	296	should be ....
8.	τριακόσια σαράντα τέσσερα	434	should be ....

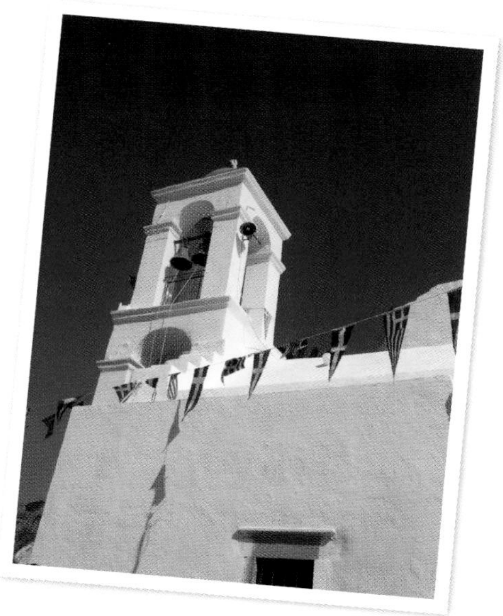

Μπορείτε να με βοηθήσετε;
A bit of help

12

In this unit we've put together an essential survival kit, to cover any situations in which you might run into problems.

Traveller's tip

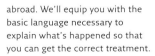

One of the problems often spoken about by students of Greek is the notion that Greeks talk much more quickly than speakers of English, and that regional accents can be hard to follow. It's a fact that accents from the south of the country tend to be more difficult to understand, as various letters and word-endings seem to be missed off. The speed issue may or may not be true, but it's inevitable that there will be times when you don't catch what's been said to you, so we're going to focus on a few expressions to make it clear that you haven't understood, to ask for repetitions, and so on.

It's fair to say that Greece is generally a safe, friendly and easy-going place to spend time, but in any city or country there will always be the minority element looking to pick your pocket or trick you in some way. We'll show you what you need to say if you've lost your passport, money, etc.

Equally, there's no legislating for when illness can strike, at home or abroad. We'll equip you with the basic language necessary to explain what's happened so that you can get the correct treatment.

If during your visit to Greece you become ill, the first step is to go to the local pharmacy. Chemists are qualified to give advice and treatment for minor problems such as coughs, colds, minor injuries, insect bites, etc. Pharmacies are closed on Saturdays, but there is a normally a rota displayed on the pharmacy's window with the opening times for an after-hours service and for weekends.

In this unit, as well as focusing on situation-specific language, we'll dip briefly into the past tense so that you can say what has already happened, for example: 'I've lost my passport'**Έχασα το διαβατήριό μου**, or 'My wallet has been stolen' **Μου έκλεψαν το πορτοφόλι**.

Listen up 1

Here is a dialogue between a tourist and a police officer. The tourist is explaining that he has lost his rucksack. 70

Words and phrases 1

έχασα (χάνω)	to lose
ο σάκκος	the rucksack
νομίζω	I think
σήμερα	today
η παραλία	the beach
μήπως	perhaps
Μπορείτε να τον περιγράψετε;	Can you describe it?
μέσα	inside
το πορτοφόλι	the wallet/purse
το χαρτονόμισμα/τα χαρτονομίσματα	the banknote/the banknotes
το κέρμα/τα κέρματα	the coin/the coins
τα γυαλιά	the glasses
το κινητό	the mobile phone
το κλειδί/τα κλειδιά	the key/the keys

Μπορείτε να σύμπληρώσετε ...	Can you fill in ...
η φόρμα	the form
εντάξει	OK
Θα σας ειδοποιήσουμε.	We will let you know.
αν	if
βρούμε (βρίσκω)	to find

Unlocking the language 1

In this section we will learn some basic verbs in the past tense, such as 'I was', 'I had', 'I lost', 'I went', 'I ate', 'I drank'. As most of the basic verbs are irregular it is simpler to learn how each one of them is conjugated.

to be		to have		to lose	
I was	ήμουν	I had	είχα	I lost	έχασα
you were	ήσουν	you had	είχες	you lost	έχασες
he/she was	ήταν	he/she had	είχε	he/she lost	έχασε
we were	είμασταν	we had	είχαμε	we lost	χάσαμε
you were	είσασταν	you had	είχατε	you lost	χάσατε
they were	ήτανε	they had	είχαν	they lost	έχασαν

to go		to eat		to drink	
I went	πήγα	I ate	έφαγα	I drank	ήπια
you went	πήγες	you ate	έφαγες	you drank	ήπιες
he/she went	πήγε	he/she ate	έφαγε	he/she drank	ήπιε
we went	πήγαμε	we ate	φάγαμε	we drank	ήπιαμε
you went	πήγατε	you ate	φάγατε	you drank	ήπιατε
they went	πήγαν	they ate	έφαγαν	they drank	ήπιαν

Your turn 1

Check your understanding. Select the correct answer: 70

1. The tourist lost his:
   a. rucksack
   b. suitcase
   c. friend

2. In his wallet there were:
   a. 15 euros in banknotes and 5 euros in coins
   b. 50 euros in banknotes and 15 euros in coins
   c. 50 euros in banknotes and 5 euros in coins

3. Among the things he lost were:
   a. his passport and house keys
   b. his passport and hotel keys
   c. his glasses and house keys

Find expressions in the dialogue that convey the following: 70

1. Where did you lose it and when?
2. What was inside?
3. I think I lost it this morning.
4. Can you fill in this form?
5. With pleasure.
6. We will let you know if we find it.

Pronunciation Tip

Be careful when stressing words. Stressing the wrong syllable can lead in misunderstandings as the word may have a totally different meaning, for example: **ποτέ** means 'never' but **πότε** means 'when'.

How would you say the following in Greek? Check your answers by listening to the audio track. 71

1. I lost my passport.
2. My wallet had 20 euros in it.
3. I lost my keys and my glasses.
4. My mobile is black.

Listen to the dialogue and circle the correct answer: 72

1. The tourist lost:
   a. his mobile
   b. his wallet
   c. his bag
2. He lost it this morning:
   a. on the beach
   b. at the café
   c. at the swimming pool
3. It is:
   a. small, red, made out of leather
   b. small, brown, made out of leather
   c. small, green, made out of leather
4. Inside there were:
   a. 13 euros
   b. 30 euros
   c. 35 euros

Match the words with the pictures:

1. γυαλιά
2. κλειδιά
3. διαβατήριο
4. κινητό
5. σάκκος
6. πορτοφόλι

a. 

b. 

c. 

d. 

e. 

f. 

Listen up 2

Peter is not feeling very well and has decided to go to see the doctor. Listen to the dialogue. Words and phrases 2 sets out the new vocabulary you'll hear on the audio track. 73

Words and phrases 2

αισθάνομαι	to feel
Από πότε;	Since when?
χτες	yesterday
το σύμπτωμα/τα συμπτώματα	the symptom/the symptoms
πονάω	to ache
το κεφάλι	the head
ο λαιμός	the throat
βήχω	to cough
ο πυρετός	the fever
το κρυολόγημα	the cold (illness)
το παυσίπονο	the painkiller
το χάπι/τα χάπια	the tablet/the tablets
το σιρόπι	the syrup
Κάθε πότε;	How often?
οφείλω	to owe
η ασφάλεια	the insurance
δωρεάν	free of charge

Unlocking the language 2

In this section we will learn how to use possessive pronouns in Greek. It's very straightforward. Possessive pronouns are the words we use to indicate possession: my, your, his, her, our, your, their. In Greek, they are: **μου** (my), **σου** (your), **του** (his), **της** (her), **μας** (our), **σας** (your), **τους** (their). In English, the possessive pronoun precedes the noun, for example: my father, your uncle, her mother, etc. In Greek, however, the possessive pronoun follows the noun: **ο πατέρας μου, ο θείος σου, η μητέρα της**.

Pronunciation Tip

The combination letters '**αι**', '**ου**', '**οι**' and '**ει**' sound like '**ε**', '**oo**', '**ι**' and '**ι**' respectively. If you want to pronounce them as separate letters, you need to put two little dots '¨' on the '**ι**'. For example: in the word **πονόλαιμος** the '**αι**' sounds like an '**ε**', but in the word **ευρωπαϊκή** it sounds like a separate '**α**' and '**ι**'.

Your turn 2

Check your understanding. True or false? 73

		True	False
1.	The patient has fever.	☐	☐
2.	He has been unwell since yesterday morning.	☐	☐
3.	He should stay in bed for two to three days.	☐	☐

Find expressions in the dialogue that convey the following: 73

1. I don't feel well.
2. What are the symptoms?
3. Have you got a fever?
4. How much do I owe you?
5. Have you got insurance?
6. It is free.

Tip

When talking about aches and pains there are two ways of expressing them. You can either say:

Πονάει το κεφάλι μου or **έχω πονοκέφαλο**
Πονάει ο λαιμός μου or **έχω πονόλαιμο**
Πονάει η κοιλιά μου or **έχω πονόκοιλο** (tummy ache)
Πονάει το δόντι μου or **έχω πονόδοντο** (toothache)

How would you say the following in Greek? Check your answers by listening to the audio track. 74

1. I have a headache.
2. I have a sore throat.
3. I have a temperature.
4. since yesterday

Listen to the dialogue and say whether the following statements are true or false: 75

		True	False
1.	The patient has felt unwell since yesterday evening.	☐	☐
2.	He has a sore throat.	☐	☐
3.	He has fever.	☐	☐
4.	He should take a cough syrup three times a day for a couple of days.	☐	☐

Match the words with the pictures:

1. σιρόπι
2. Ευρωπαϊκή Κάρτα Υγείας
3. θερμόμετρο
4. χάπια

a. 

b. 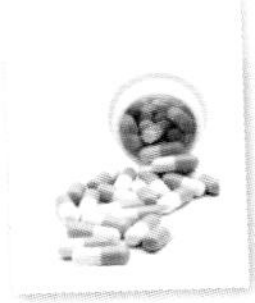

c. 

d. 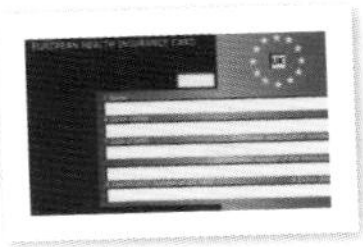

Let's recap

Here are some more activities to practise what you've learnt in this unit.

Match the words with the pictures:

1. πονάει το κεφάλι μου
2. έχω πονόλαιμο
3. βήχω
4. έχω πυρετό

a. 

b. 

c. 

d. 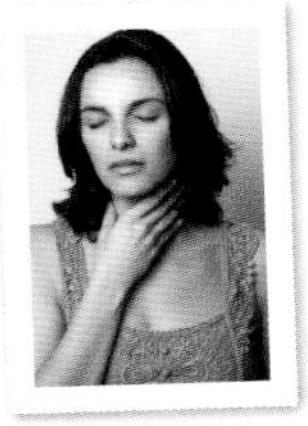

Put the words of the following sentences in the correct order:

1. λαιμός πονάει μου ο ....
2. συμπτώματα έχετε τι ....
3. σιρόπι μέρες πάρτε γιά αυτό δύο το ....
4. το μου έχασα γυαλιά τα και πισίνα πορτοφόλι στην μου ....

....

HAVE YOU SEEN OUR FULL GREEK RANGE? PICK A TITLE TO FIT YOUR LEARNING STYLE.

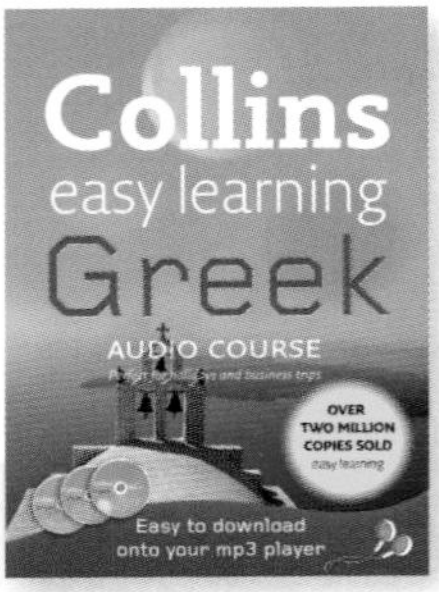

Audio Course
£14.99

Collins Easy Learning Audio Courses

This exciting course allows learners to absorb the basics at home or on the move, without the need for thick textbooks or complex grammar.

Collins Phrasebooks

These portable, easy-to-use phrasebooks will ensure you get the right word – every time.

Gem Phrasebook
£4.50

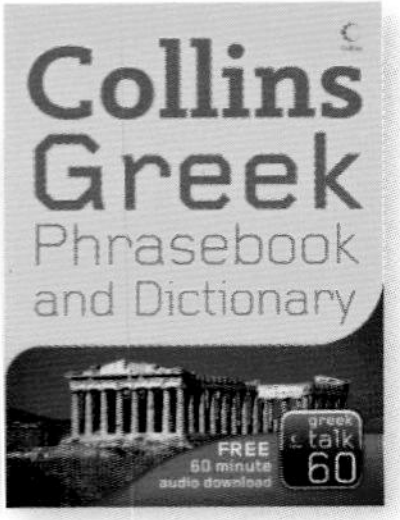

Phrasebook and Dictionary
£4.99

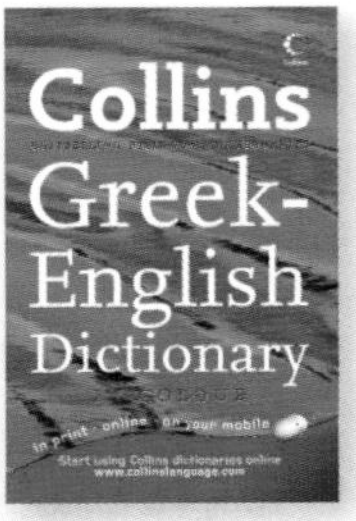

Greek-English Dictionary
£20

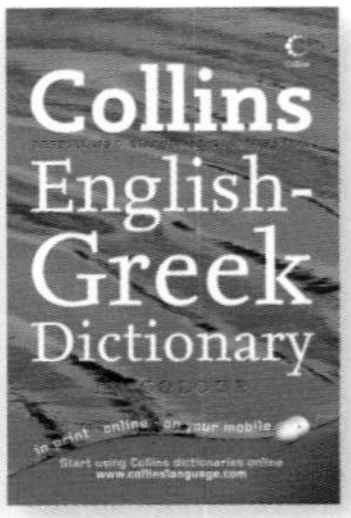

English-Greek Dictionary
£20

Gem Greek Dictionary
£5.99

Collins Dictionaries

Our bestselling dictionaries help you take you learning to the next level.

Collins products are available from all good bookshops nationwide.
For further information visit: www.collinslanguage.com

Collins